ENTER AT YOUR OWN RISK

WALLACE HENLEY

ENTER AT YOUR OWN RISK

FLEMING H. REVELL COMPANY

OLD TAPPAN, NEW JERSEY

Scripture quotations identified KJV are from the King James Version of the Bible.

Scripture quotations identified NEB are from *The New English Bible.* © The Delegates of the Oxford University Press and The Syndics of the Cambridge University Press 1961, 1970. Reprinted by permission.

Excerpts from *Conflict and Conscience* are by Mark Hatfield, published by Word Books, Waco, Texas, 1971. Used by permission.

Library of Congress Cataloging in Publication Data

Henley, Wallace.
    Enter at your own risk.

      1.   Christian life—Baptist authors.   I.   Title.
BV4501.2.H373   248'.48'61   74–11028
ISBN 0–8007–0686–2

TO
Irene,
for taking the risks.

CONTENTS

PREFACE

"Build your cities under Vesuvius!" Friedrich Nietzsche, the German philosopher who penned that stark imperative of risk, would flip in his grave if he knew that someone would suggest that he may have unwittingly captured the real character of Christian discipleship. Nietzsche's theology looked very much like a ball of yarn after being assaulted by a whole family of cats. It was Nietzsche, writing in the nineteenth century, who would lay important foundations for the God-is-dead movement which would become fashionable for a brief flash during the twentieth century.

Yet to be a follower of Jesus Christ is something like building a life under a seething, bubbling volcano. Christian discipleship is an incredibly risky business.

Let me erect a billboard right here though, reading like this: It is far riskier *not* to be a disciple of Christ. The promises of God are as stable and as certain as granite. But living daily a discipleship consistent with the boldness in claiming those promises is where the matter gets risky.

The compulsion for writing this book is a highly personal one. It stems from my own dissatisfaction with my witness for Christ. I have found that too often I have contented myself with delightful dreams (based on reality) about the fulfillment of God's promises, while neglecting to put my life on the line for Christ to the extent that I take some genuine risks. I have wanted resurrection without crucifixion, heaven without a pilgrimage. It doesn't work that way.

I began this book when I was the religion editor of *The Birmingham News,* a moderately large daily newspaper. I had covered, over a three-year period, most of the national conclaves of the major denominations. Frankly, the meetings were beginning to sour me—an ordained minister—on the church. What I saw at the national conventions was one vast stab at survival. I felt the churches were trying to stay alive when they should have left their survival in the hands of God, and majored their efforts on carrying out His mission no matter what the cost.

I still believe that, except somewhere between the beginning and ending of this book, something happened to me. It occurred to me that *I* was what was wrong with the church. It was my cowardice, my lack of willingness to risk everything in the mission of Christ that was amplified and multiplied in the collective body we designate as "church." For it is composed of all of us individual "churches," and the collective body will be no more bold in its mission than we are individually.

So I got turned on about the church again. I am even more exuberant and excited about it than I was in my seminary days, when I thought nothing could blunt my enthusiasm. Perhaps it took those years in which I stood around on its periphery as a mere spectator. I went from laborer to news-paperman to presidential assistant, and the big lesson I emerged with is that, as Findley Edge has put it, the church is where the action is. That action has to be carried out in boldness, and it has to be directed toward the world.

After all, I found the secularists were pretty bold in doing whatever they were doing with the world. Some of the boldest people I know are insurance men. There is little lacking in the heroism of some of the radical and violent revolutionaries of our day. Boldness has become such a thing that people have no reluctance to happily announce themselves Satan-worshipers, followers of Zen, and down-right brazen disciples of teen-age gurus from India. Disciples of Jesus have got to get as bold as was Peter when he stood after Pentecost to preach in a city where they wanted his head!

This gets us to the roots of our faith. There's nothing to be ashamed of in the family tree of Christendom. It is made up of men like Peter, Paul, Stephen, and countless others who risked everything to do the work of Christ in the world. In fact, if they hadn't, no one would be writing and talking about discipleship today. There wouldn't be any Christians, no followers of Jesus. God could have chosen nature, the stones, all kinds of means of getting across His message of reconciliation between God and man and between men. But He chose men. He called us, not to live quaking, trembling lives, but heroic, bold-risk lives.

Just look at the way we get into the Kingdom. Faith is an act of boldness. It is placing your life in the care of something, or someone, to the extent that if they fail, you lose your life! It's like committing yourself to an airplane. So being a Christian is giving yourself so completely to God that if He were to fail (which He won't), not only would you lose your physical existence, but your very being.

Being committed to Christ is turning one's life over to a Carpenter who said He was God. It is putting that which is most precious to a person in the care of Someone we've never seen. It is living an entire life under the guidance of a Book written over centuries by hundreds of different writers, miraculously held to the point by the Spirit of God. To be a Christian *is* an act of boldness!

One of the great quests of man has been to try to prove the existence of God. Because it couldn't be visibly observed in the ancient alchemists's lab, or in modern mathematical formulas, or in test tubes, men have sometimes concluded that God doesn't exist. But they were centering their search in the wrong area (though God *is* revealed in scientists' labs, since there is a partial revelation of Himself in nature). The real proof of the pudding is in the lives of people, and most completely in Jesus, the Son of God, the full and absolute revelation of God.

Our faith is not really the flimsy thing I may have made it sound. Just look at the way God has moved in the lives of His people for the evidence of its strength and vitality. I think of those in my own experience: Irene, my wife, who has followed me from pole to pole, exuberant and as believing and willing to risk as ever. There's John Haggai, a disciple of Christ whom I honestly believe would be distributing Gospel tracts to the lion keepers as he was led into the arena! I think of Dr. Kyung Chik Han, pastor-emeritus of Yung Nak Presbyterian Church in Seoul, Korea, who refused to be spooked by either Japanese or North Korean invaders. And, heavenly days, one of the leaders of this list would have to be my Uncle Redus Vasser—about whom I will write later. I could go on and on, naming people whose bold living for Christ has sparked the fires within me. These people cover the gamut in style of witness. But they share one thing in common: They believe in Jesus Christ so thoroughly that they've put the totality of their lives on Him, risking everything.

If the bulk of Jesus' disciples could recover heroism and boldness and the willingness to risk, this world would be as shaken by the Christian faith as it was in the first three centuries after Jesus' Resurrection. I sincerely believe that it could happen here and now. I have enumerated here only a few of the risks awaiting the disciple of Christ. There are many more. If we are willing to take them, the world—the entire world—can be changed!

1

THE RISK OF OPENNESS

Charlie was known in our neighborhood as an imbecile —the village idiot, if you will. But it wasn't true. He may have been tongue-tied, and the brain in his adult body was definitely infantile. But Charlie taught me a basic lesson about Christian discipleship. He helped me see that the Christian experience is not a cracker, which has to be pre-served in an airtight wrapper. Rather, the command of Jesus is that His disciples live precariously open lives; that they risk being so open that if outside circumstances and other people threaten to wilt them, they don't retreat to the cracker box, but remain out there in the open. Charlie taught me that.

Charlie's unconscious tutoring program began for me when I joined the staff of a large and, I smugly thought, prestigious church. Our sanctuary was a vast, gilded cavern, a sure-enough Baptist cathedral!

One Sunday morning, shortly after going to work there, I was to give the invocation. That meant I got to sit on the platform. I strode in with the other ministers, trying to look tall (at five-seven, quite a struggle) and ministerial. We were well into the service when, in a squint, I could see a stumpy little hobo with a Charlie Chaplin shuffle coming into the sanctuary. The air conditioning was in mortal combat with one of the hottest summers I had ever experienced, but the little character coming into our church wore a grease-stained overcoat which would have shamed Freddie the Freeloader. The innocent, naïve smile of the retarded was on his face. "He's just got to stop at the back row," I thought, looking at the polished, notable folk whose eyes and noses he might assault.

But Charlie had no intention of stopping at the back row. He wanted to hear and see the preacher, and that meant being down front. So we sat, midst our readings and hymns and prayers, as Charlie baby-stepped to the second pew and made a major ceremony out of getting his greasy coat arranged and nodding to the people who were making little buffer zones between their territories and Charlie's on the pew. I couldn't figure why the ushers hadn't done more to protect the sensitivities of God's people from such intrusions.

Subconsciously, a barrier had already been erected in my mind to block out any kind of relationship with Charlie. After all, I reasoned, I had been called to minister to those who counted, not to those who could make no observable contributions in talent or wealth. To have gotten involved with Charlie would have been a waste of time, since he had nothing with which to reciprocate.

Was I ever wrong!

It began dawning on me a few Sundays later, when Charlie asked me if I would drop him off at the hovel which passed for his home. There is a weird reality to my life I cannot explain. The world's nuisances collect at my elbow like flies to flypaper. Charlie had become, in my mind, the most exasperating nuisance I had ever dealt with. I shook and shook but he clung to my elbow, smiling that simple, naïve, and so beautifully innocent smile. I arranged for someone else to drive Charlie home.

But Sunday after Sunday, Charlie bugged me. I would be in conversation with Mrs. Tinderbox, and Charlie would be dangling off my elbow, asking me to be his chauffeur. Brother Bigwallet would be bending my ear about the travails of his daughter's European jaunt, and I would be tempted to explain that, no, I didn't have a Siamese twin, that was just Charlie.

I really couldn't understand it. I always arranged for someone to take care of Charlie. He always had a ride home, driven by one of the surrogate chauffeurs I went to such lengths to retain. The thickness of my skull is, at some points, exceeded only by a Swiss bank vault, and it took me forever to get the message: It's not the surrogates Charlie wants for friendship, Dummy, it's you. He really doesn't care whether he has a ride home or not. The whole thing is a ploy to win a friend.

Once that realization bored through my senses, other revelations, however indirect, began zapping me by way of Charlie. The first thing I realized was that the Kingdom of God was made for people like Charlie, or it was made for no one. I also understood that the question of my whole ministry—its credibility and effectiveness—was tied up in whether or not I could be open to those Charlie-people.

To tell the truth, I was surprised at me. I thought I was open. I had certainly been taught better. For example, there had been the Reverend Richard Francis, a preacher I had plagued during student days as music director. I recalled the day the local drunk, whose word was as sound as an Edsel, came to see Francis because he needed three hundred dollars to make bond. I watched as Richard co-signed a bank note with the man. While I trembled a little at Richard's doing what I figured was kissing three hundred dollars good-bye, I kept saying over and over again: "That's the way it's done; being a minister is putting it all on the line for others, just like Richard is doing right now."

So why was I such an insensitive snob when it came to Charlie? Mainly, because openness is not a theoretical thing, but an experiential risk for the Christian. You can go on and on about how you've got it, but until you're cheek to cheek with whomever or whatever demands that you take the risk of being open, you really can't be sure. Sometimes you have to be pried open, like I was, with God using a guy like Charlie as the lever.

Please don't read this as Henley proclaiming how great he is. Honestly, I find that one has to face each situation demanding openness, and take the risk again and again, with each time as scary as the first. There are times when I really blow it, even after Charlie, even after Richard Francis.

Since openness is experiential rather than theoretical, most of us have little idea about what an open life really is. Fortunately, Jesus pioneered virtually every frontier of humanity's life experience, and God set patterns of openness in Him that have not been diminished in their exemplary quality by two thousand years.

In fact, nothing is so graphically illustrative nor so much a direct result of this openness than the cross. Oliver Cromwell is supposed to have told his portrait painter to depict him with all his warts. The only "wart" in the life of Jesus was the cross, and its immense shame (though the Resurrection dissolved that wart!). It was certainly a "wart" when viewed by the disciples on the uphill side of Resurrection and Pentecost. But Jesus made no attempt to conceal it!

Nor did He ever stop doing and saying the things that would make the cross inevitable. By simple silence, a retreat (permanently) to the balmy coast of the Sea of Galilee, or up into the mountains, it could have all been sidestepped. Jesus went to the coasts and mountains, all right, but it was always to open Himself a bit more to the people. What for others would have been places of seclusion were for Him arenas of stark openness.

The openness of Jesus carved a trail by which His enemies could follow and find Him, and He knew all along He was hacking out such a trail. How this openness condemns our age of ambiguity! In the palaces of the politicians, the ambiguity and double-talk is such that outright lies are labeled as mere "inoperative" statements. In 1971, after the John F. Kennedy Library opened Kennedy files to the public, a reporter for the *New York Times* came across one example which may be typical of the attitude of some in politics. It was a press release prepared by Pierre Salinger, dealing with a meeting of the cabinet concerning Vietnam. In the margin, in the handwriting of White House aide McGeorge Bundy was the notation: "Pierre: Champion! Excellent prose. No Surprise. 'A communique should say nothing in such a way as to fool the press without deceiving them.' " Later, Bundy said he had written the word "feed," rather than "fool." Maybe so, but the press often has every reason to feel it has been "fooled" by the ambiguity of the statements it receives at the hands of politicians.

During my brief tangle with politics, I learned early the importance of ambiguity and the extreme risk of openness. I had just become the press man for a White House-level group, after having served as a newspaper reporter. I was still very much the reporter when I had my first interview with a West Coast paper. The reporter asked me a question which got into the closet of our agency, wherein resided a few policy skeletons, which I brought out and showed the reporter, bone by bone. Licking his chops, the writer filed a juicy story which told all. The next day, I was on a trip to Mississippi. My boss tracked me down on the road and read me the riot act. I was certain my government career was over before it was off the ground. Ambiguity, I found—shamefully—was a lot less risky than openness.

Had Jesus been the president of the United States (or the premier of the Soviet Union, for that matter), He would have had around Him brilliant wordsmiths who could pen announcements that taxes were being raised 100 percent and still have everyone applauding and wanting to be the first to pay. To them He might have opened the possibility of the cross, and instructed them to prepare a statement. It might have read like this:

> My fellow citizens: There are rumors that I may have to go up to Jerusalem and die. Well, let Me simply say that the exigencies of the time being what they are, one should be cautioned from the expedient of opting for one course over another. Our honor will be kept intact. I am glad to clear up this matter once and for all.

But then Jesus wasn't president or premier, but Saviour of mankind, and when the cross loomed, His openness about His vulnerability to it was incredibly stark, and loaded with risk!

For all that, though, the world is not nearly so hurt by political ambiguity as it is when the people of God opt for ambiguity. Counselors to clergymen, reported Arthur Herzog in *The Church Trap,* are finding that "the pulpit today is an anxious seat." Much of that anxiety stems from the mandate on the preacher of the Gospel to apply God's Word in clear and unmistakable tones, irrespective of the threat to his survival. Ambiguity, generalizations that touch the lives of no one, too easily become the essence of the sermon under such circumstances. Researchers Rodney Stark, Bruce D. Foster, Charles Glock, and Harold Quinley analyzed the content of modern preaching in a book they pointedly called *Wayward Shepherds.* Before publication, the journal *Psychology Today* took an advance look at the book's findings. A sassy subhead with the *Psychology Today* piece summed up the sad results: "Things may come apart and the center may not hold, but you're unlikely to hear about it in the Sunday sermon at the church of your choice."

Admittedly, it's easy and perhaps a bit unfair to take potshots at preachers for not risking themselves from the security of a university post or magazine publishing house. And what Stark and company consider specific preaching may be quite different from what many ministers consider such. But we're dealing here, not with the medicine-show peddling of some quack elixir, but the very Word of God which, if man can hear clearly, will change his life! Perhaps the great need is that pastor and congregation open themselves to one another to such a degree that the Word can be preached even when it hurts. That kind of openness is risky indeed.

The cross as fact is exemplary of that openness, but there is powerful symbolism here as well. Take, for example, the splitting of the temple veil, from top to bottom. The scene is dramatic enough in its own right: the earth rumbling, sky darkening, and suddenly the loud "r-r-r-r-rip" as the thick thing is torn apart by an unseen force. But the real drama is in what the episode with the veil says about the way God relates to man. "God's presence," said W.W. Barnes in *Southwestern Sermons,* "was no longer limited to the high priest on one day of the year but was henceforth to be opened to access by any human being every day in the year for all the years. . . ."

God, then, doesn't open Himself to bespectacled astronomers and close Himself to plumbers. He is not one to show up for black-frocked priests and stay at home for gray-flanneled accountants. Nor is He a deity who reveals Himself to white-headed Solomons and hides from giggling high-school sophomores. If the tearing of the temple veil means nothing else, it is a clear sign that God is not selective about whom He lets get to know Him.

The cross, of course, would not have been possible without the incarnation of God in the person of Jesus. Incarnation itself says volumes about the way God opens Himself to man.

Hardly anyone got a greater kick out of talking about incarnation than did John. Maybe we don't get the concussion this far removed from Greek classical thought, but John must have delighted in exploding little philosophical bombshells. In the first chapter of his Gospel, John wrote about the *Logos*—the "Word"—being one and the same as God Himself. The Logos as a concept wasn't foreign to the Jews and Greeks of John's day. But here's where the bomb burst comes: For both the Jews and Greeks, the Logos was a principle by which man could have an indirect relationship with God. It was unthinkable that the Logos and God might be identical. For the Jews, God was so remotely transcendent that His name couldn't even be pronounced. For the Greeks, the material universe, including man, was so evil that no direct link between it and God could possibly exist. So, for both Jews and Greeks, the Logos was a neat means of getting to God without dirtying the heavenly throne.

Then John came saying that God had opened Himself to man so thoroughly that He was the Logos, not disclosing information about some third party but revealing Himself! And later, the Logos made flesh would say, ". . . he that hath seen me hath seen the Father . . ." (John 14:9 KJV). If John had been writing in the days since Marconi, he might have illustrated his point with the wireless radio, for the Jews and Greeks hoping to learn about God via an indirect principle were like a person trying to learn about Franklin D. Roosevelt by listening to his "Fireside Chats." When John said that the Logos and God were identical, it would be as if the radio transmitter turned into FDR!

With the scratches of his stylus, John exploded the myth that God, to paraphrase George Buttrick, had left the running of the universe to some demiurge while He holed up in some Shangri-la of tranquility. John was saying that when the voice cried in Eden to Adam: "Where art thou?" (Genesis 3:9 KJV), it was not a posse or a search party, but God Himself. And in that, He was opening up His love and concern and compassion for a fickle creature called man. It is the same now, only the voice beckons midst bombs exploding in Indochina, midst screaming mobs in the Middle East, midst the private neurosis of a young stockbroker, and midst the chamber of silent loneliness surrounding an old woman. He is here, and He is making no attempt to be anything other than completely open.

Despite such an overpowering set of examples from my Master, I still had trouble opening to Charlie. It comes back to the point of a moment ago: Openness is not theoretical, but experiential. In trying to get my life open to Charlie, I discovered there was a first step, namely, that I had to be open to myself. Just admitting that I might have lied to me about myself hurt. But it was a risk I had to take, for, if a person can't take a hard look at his own exposed vulnerable being and concede his limitations, he can never know the infinite possibilities of God's corrective actions in his life. Such a person lives forever on the petty assumption that what he perceives of himself he likes, and that is enough. We never get to the core of what we can be until we take the risk of opening ourselves *to* ourselves.

For years, my father struggled with alcoholism. I have sorted through the tangle of possible causes for his problem again and again since his death in 1966 in a mental institution. I cannot decipher all the causes, but this I know: He couldn't stop drinking because somehow he couldn't open himself to himself and concede the existence of the problem. I attempted—clumsily, no doubt—every form of confrontation I knew to make him see his need. But always he would reply, "I'm not drinking; I do not drink"—that despite the fact that one night I tried to help him back to his house (he and my mother had long since divorced), and had to battle to keep him from falling. Still he refused to open up. I reached into his pocket and pulled out a partially drained fifth. "How did that get there?" he asked.

The mental factors that prohibited him from opening up I will have to leave to the psychologists. But certainly one of the factors would have been the fact that such an opening would have brought the risk of having to face personal limitations, and whatever was wrong with my father made it necessary for him to blind himself to such stark self-honesty.

The self-opening process is at its riskiest when it forces us to that ultimate concession: "I am sinner." This is an incredibly difficult admission for modern man, whose ploys of concealing the truth about himself from himself reach the limits of sophistication. Shakespeare, in his *Julius Caesar,* told it like it was (and is) when he penned: "The fault, dear Brutus, is not in our stars, but in ourselves. . . ." Despite such admonitions, we men remain gung ho for the cover-up. White Houses and Pentagons and political hacks aren't the only artisans of the cover-up. It is a universal practice, carried on at the most intimate level of the human being, that part of a man that keeps wanting to acknowledge the existence of human limitation, of sin.

We like to say, for example, that our devilment is the result of our environment. Anyone who had a happy childhood is in sad shape nowadays, since the major rationale for our shoddy behavior is our upbringing. We lament our failure to adjust to our environment, never realizing that the environment to which we have failed to "adjust" is the Kingdom of God. *Homo sapiens* has a mad penchant for screaming about the abuse of the environment as if it had been done by some extraterrestrial force, and somehow misses the New Testament point that what has dominion over man determines how man exercises his dominion over creation.

Richard L. Means has written about the "crisis in American values" in *The Ethical Imperative.* He notes there is a common assumption that we are experiencing a "breakdown of values," but that "our social scientists, committed to an ideal of objective neutrality, are most reluctant to venture into the realm of ethics." As much as anything, this is what the "crisis in values" is all about. It hangs on the failure of students of our society and observers in general, who do exhaustive critiques, to point toward something better. They have been well trained in the techniques of criticism, but want to sidestep the more demanding job of committing themselves to pointing directions. That, of course, would also mean that such social scientists would have to open up to themselves, and see that they, as individual people, are part of that vast abstraction known as "society." The Christian, however, can't afford the luxurious cop-out known as "objective neutrality," and abandoning that stance brings the risk of that ultimate self-openness, the concession that "I am sinner."

Just about the time a person gets into the morbid valley of that depressing bit of self-realization, the light breaks through, for the ultimate concession can lead to the ultimate confession: Jesus Christ is Lord. Now the openness moves from a one-man act to, well, dialogue. And the dialogue by which a person can eventually learn to be open to all people starts with God.

The most significant fact in all this business about openness is that it is God who cracks the ice about Himself. When God opens Himself to us, it is just that. He is not shedding light on new creeds nor on more expansive dogma nor more noble chitchat. He is putting the light on Himself. Richard Niebuhr, in his classical study *The Meaning of Revelation,* says:

Selves cannot be discovered as America was found by Columbus, by sailing in the direction of a secret and a

guess; this new continent must come to us or remain unknown.

The Bible is the history of God gradually lifting the veil from
Himself (*revelation* means the removal of a veil). It comes
up inch by inch, says the author of Hebrews—first a mite
of revelation through the ancients, then the full disclosure
through Jesus the Christ.

Had God not taken this initiative, we mortals would have
had no choice but to peg the events of our lives to "fate,"
or some such impersonal force. The astrologers would have
become our kings. Or, we would have been like Sartre, in
that photo *Life* magazine ran to illustrate an article on his
bleak existentialist outlook. In the picture, Sartre is standing
on a tiny ice floe in the middle of a chilly stream. He is
alone, as he perceives man to be in the universe, at the
mercy of impersonal forces. But Sartre's pantomine does
not represent accurately man in the cosmos. For the truth
of revelation is that God has voluntarily opened Himself to
man, and there is no cosmic loneliness!

We don't have to bribe God to open to us. Rather, as in
that immortal sermon "The Hound of Heaven," God is
pursuing the humanity He loves. *He* shatters the silence
after man's disastrous choices in Eden; *He* breaks through
the darkness of Sinai to to give Moses the Law; *He* dons the
paltry clothing of human flesh so that we might know Him
personally.

Since God takes the onus of opening to us, it's obvious
He wants something to do with us. In fact, this involvement
of God with us in the human epic is the sum total of history.
No one has defined *history* better than George Buttrick
when he says, in *Christ and History,* that it "is Dialogue

between God and man-in-pilgrimage in the language of
Event; and Christ is the Conversation's middle term, the key
to the translation, the light in which the whole pilgrimage
can be seen and understood and the love in which history's
brokenness is healed."

If Christ is to be that definitive "middle term" in the
"conversation" between God and man, then His involvement with us must be open in its character. He cannot be
the anonymous do-gooder who dribbles ointment on our
wounds, then withdraws before we regain consciousness.
Everyone admires the guy who contributes, anonymously,
the cash to save us at the last minute. But Jesus is here in
history to save us, and if He's to perform that mission suc-
cessfully, then His participation with us must be open. For,
as Buttrick says, our redemption must come both from
within and beyond history. Within, because we are free,
and the choice must be made in the light of our human
environment. Our salvation must come simultaneously from
beyond history because all of human history is consumed
by the same sickness. But if we see our Redeemer and do
not know Him, we will merely see His suffering and conclude that He is just another poor sucker like us, powerless
to rise out of the human dilemma.

That is, after all, the predicament of all the false saviours
we look to: they are as powerless as we are. But Jesus the
Christ is for real, He is genuine, and the glory of it is that He
doesn't come with TOP SECRET stamped on His forehead. He
opens Himself to us so that we will know, all at once, that
He is one of us, yet not one of us. Buttrick asks, "Is Jesus
in history? If He is not, if He only mimics our human life
. . . if thus His temptations were only shadowboxing and His
Cross a fiction, He is not redemption, but almost an insult

to our pain." But we know He is no insult, for His open vulnerability has shown us His temptation was not shadow-boxing nor His cross fiction. And the same open participation with us in the here and now has shown us there is no pipe-dreaming to His Resurrection, either.

Thus, as we open ourselves to ourselves and run to the abyss of the confession of our sinfulness, the hand we see reaching out to lift us across the chasm is God's. We see and know Him and understand His strength because He lets us *In His time* know Him. God opens Himself to man that man might be fully open.

To what? Obviously, to himself and to God. But how is this openness to God best expressed? There can be only one answer, spelled out, again, in the example of Jesus: The way we express our openness to God is to risk being open to other people, the Charlie-types and all others.

Early in my ministry, I had decided I was God's gift to the cosmos, and that the world merely awaited the twittering of my vocal cords. I was serving in a church whose community contained an equal number of poor and affluent. They were separated by the normal barriers. For some reason—noble, I hope—I decided I would plunge into saving the poor. I selected a government housing project near the church, and began a program of calling on every apartment.

My plan was to do a one-shot visit, plant the seed, and see what would happen—which was a grand total of nothing. I did note, however, that some of these folk needed a minister—on a continuing basis—and it appeared to them I had volunteered. Gradually, I found myself being drawn into their misery. Mr. and Mrs. Smith were on the verge of divorce again because he was on an endless drunk and couldn't get any work; Mr. Rivers was near death with a stomach cancer and his elderly wife needed some help in getting him to the hospital; Mrs. Reeves, imprisoned in her bed, horribly disfigured by childhood disease, was beaten regularly by some fiend she was convinced loved her anyway. We plodded through these scenarios of agony for six months before I realized these people were begging me to be *open to their pain.*

Our human tendency is that when we do open ourselves to other people, it is usually on a highly selective basis. Such selectivity blots out certain people altogether. ("Steer clear of Jim; he's poison.") Even with those to whom we open ourselves, we permit openness only to certain facets of their lives. But the person who follows the Christ who was incarnate midst all the pain and tragedy of humanity finds he has an outright mandate from his Master to open up to the pain and sorrow of other people!

Such openness would make a huge difference in the way we relate to other people *and* ourselves. In the same community as the housing project and all its hurt, lived the world's most beleaguered hypochondriac. Call her, for our purposes here, Mrs. Robinson. One afternoon, she called me to brief me (roughly the equivalent of a three-hour briefing on national security) on her latest ailment, which was swelling of the feet. I bit my tongue, squelching the temptation to tell her that most people standing five-two and weighing four hundred pounds tend to foot swelling from time to time. I often thought that Mrs. Robinson might find relief from her chronic neurosis if she lost herself in the far greater needs of the housing project. But then there may have been some pain, like rejection, that made Mrs. Robinson behave the way she did. And if I were true to my Pacesetter, Jesus, I could turn her off no more than I could the sorrowful folk in the housing project!

It seems, too, that if we could become open to the pain of other people, it would make us less inclined to cause them pain. I think specifically of the church, at the moment, since we're all supposed to be there as one great "loverly" family. We are human beings, of course, and often find the church is the place where people are most vulnerable to pain. But I can't help but wonder what would happen in all those church battles I've seen if the people on the various sides of the squabbles had bent themselves in determination to spare their "enemies" pain. Maybe this is what Jesus means when He tells us to turn the other cheek (*see* Luke 6:29). If we are all in the community of Christ (the church), and we are all open to the pain of others in that community, then all cheek-slapping is going to stop after a while, in the community of Christ at least. But shouldn't it cease there first? Can we expect it to stop anywhere in the social order if it doesn't cease in God's church?

While it is true there are some benefits from opening to the pain of others (like the cessation of cheek-slapping and the demise of Mrs. Robinson's neurosis), it must be red-lettered that there is immense risk—namely, the person opening to the pain of others is likely to get hurt himself. But there is another axiom: The Christian may not be able to minister to the needs of others until he himself gets hurt. Some anonymous poet understood this truth:

Wounds must heal wounds.
The wounded seek refuge with the wounded.
There they are understood, and that by itself means a lot.

There is another aspect of this openness to others, and it is the fact that the Christian must risk being *open to the possibilities* in other people. How can this be risky? It may mean that some of life's most cherished prejudices will have to be junked. It may bring the temptation to feel threatened by abilities in others we might like to have for ourselves.

Professor Henry Higgins heard the tangled cockney of Eliza Doolittle and commented that "her kerbstone English will keep her in the gutter to the end of her days." Days never pass without that kind of comment, in some form, or some other cultural context, being uttered about someone. The poor soul may be a lame-brain student, or a bumbling worker. That person may be a secretary who can't spell "cat," and who lacks the physical endowments to make up for the professional inadequacies. So, the person is tossed on the discard heap of society, bearing the big label, NO POSSIBILITIES.

Once in my zigzagging vocational pilgrimage, I worked in a box factory. I was the highly skilled worker who crouched like a baseball catcher at the other end of a box stitcher to catch the flat, future boxes as they were spat out, all stitched together. Occasionally, the fellow who fed the cardboard into the machine would go mad and insert the material crooked. What would come out would be the most disastrous hybrid cardboard and metal could ever conceive. There would be no choice but to throw the Frankenstein boxes into a big pile which went into the burner.

All around us, there are people who have decided, or about whom it has been decided, that they got fed into the machine wrong. We say that they were behind the door when the brains got passed out, and all sorts of jabbing little accusations. Living with that attitude, or knowing that others have it, can lead a person into the hopelessness expressed by a New Yorker in his suicide note: "I'm just a peanut in Yankee Stadium, so I'm going to step on myself and end it all."

Because of the cross, however, there is no such thing as a person without possibilities. And the mandate on the Christian is not to major on seeking out the possibilities of what others may do for us, but to help others see the possibilities of what they can become. Some of these "others" may be barred from country clubs, excluded from fraternities and sororities, and even from the memberships of some churches—but they can become members of the family of God!

Since it is true that Jesus went to the cross for everybody, then it is equally true that everybody has possibilities. They may be short on talents, lean on wisdom, and poor as a peasant, but Jesus saw their possibilities and died for them. Jesus came, not only to die, but to define what we all can become, through Him. He not only *prescribes,* but *describes* as well. A major part of the Christian mission is to put out the message of that description, so that all people may realize the possibilities Christ has outlined.

That requires a lot of believing in people, and that's another place where this business of being open to their possibilities gets risky. It is the danger of winding up with the egg-splattered face of Don Quixote. Quixote was thought of as a fool by most of those who saw him in Cervantes's tale. Among other things, the old man, in his delusion, fixed on a barmaid for his chosen lady. She was a prostitute, a foulmouth, a genuine wench—maybe even the archetype of all wenches. But Quixote persisted in believing she was "Dulcinea," the epitome of beauty and innocence. She kept insisting that she was Aldonza, louse par excellence. At the end of the old fellow's life, however, Aldonza came to his bedside, pleading that he call her "Dulcinea" again. His persistent belief in the possibilities in her convinced her there really was a Dulcinea under Aldonza's pawed-over skin.

Nevertheless, Quixote was known as being loco. If we as Christians open ourselves to the God-planted possibilities in people, and strive to help them achieve those possibilities, we probably will wind up, now and then, looking like genuine suckers.

Openness with others is not a one-way street, and here especially the risk gets sticky. The open life is not one that permits us to be open to the pain and possibilities in others while permitting us to live closed lives before them. To come the full circle, and to insure that openness is complete, the Christian is commanded to open his life to others so that they may receive him, as he receives them.

It is critical that anyone hoping to minister in the name of Christ be as open as possible about himself, before those toward whom he aims his ministry. The importance of this is underscored in the contrast between two pastors I know. The first I will describe, in kindness, as an "alien" minister. He is one of Christendom's best front men. He is plenty open in receiving and understanding his people. His preaching shows he believes in their possibilities; he counsels them and opens himself to their pain. But so far as the people are concerned, he is a phantom. To every person, he gives the same glossed-over ministerial smile, or, when required, look of sadness. The people whose lives he is trying to touch know nothing of his pain. To see him in a sport shirt at a party, or working at a hobby, or just showing frustration, would be a shocking novelty to his people. Not long ago, one of his parishioners, whom I happen to know, had a serious emotional problem. She didn't go to her pastor for help, however, but sought out an assistant minister. The reason: she said she just couldn't conceive of the senior pastor being able to identify with the problem she was having. As far as she was concerned, he was an alien to her and her kind of anxiety. The man is so remote, his ability to lead is as much in question as his ability to counsel.

Findley Edge, in his superb book on church renewal *The Greening of the Church,* considers self-disclosing openness absolutely vital. On occasion, in preaching, says Dr. Edge, the minister ought to share his own search and struggles, along with failures and discoveries. But Dr. Edge also sees the risk in such an open ministry:

> In doing this the preacher becomes exceedingly vulnerable. He runs the risk of destroying the symbol of perfection which some members unconsciously build up around him. Thus he becomes exposed as a human being with problems, weaknesses and strivings. He confesses his humanity by sometimes having to say to people, "I don't know." But in becoming more personal and more human he becomes more real for the members. They will listen to him because they can identify with his struggles. He is searching as they are.

This is very much like the other preacher I know. Not only is he open to his people, but he permits them to know him, not just through his preaching, but through his whole life-style. He goes fishing with his men. He attends costume parties with his young people. He is that one *among them* who has been called as their spiritual leader. I honestly believe the man could love his people into doing anything the Lord commands, no matter how demanding.

I've been talking here about professional clergymen. But

every follower of Jesus is called to minister, just as much as the guy who stands in the pulpit each week. The lay person doing ministry must risk openness as starkly and courageously as a fellow with "Reverend" tacked in front of his name.

Chuck Farmer is a lay person who has made a whole ministry out of risky openness. To look at Chuck, you might conclude that he is a stevedore or a tough cop. Chuck was a commercial artist by trade, who began to feel an overwhelming burden for juvenile delinquents and teen-agers in general. He especially was concerned about kids from broken homes. Chuck had no wealth. But he knew Christ and he had himself to offer. Through the generosity of some Christian businessmen and a few churches, Chuck rented a run-down house on the perimeter of a low-rent housing area in Birmingham. He established a program called "Outreach," which was essentially a vehicle for Chuck to open himself to all the kids in the community. He taught them his trade; he became a stand-in father; he took hours with the youngsters, explaining and recalling his own mistakes. Chuck isn't an orator or a scholarly teacher, so he is giving the kids what he has, an open life. Many of them are finding Christ because Chuck teaches them that what he does he does by the love of Christ. His very life is a sermon to the youngsters. Not long after Chuck began his ministry, the Birmingham police were reporting a marked drop in juvenile crime in the neighborhood where Chuck was working.

Outreach has grown now. It reaches many communities and knows no racial or economic barriers. Chuck has a staff which uses the same strategy of work he does. They simply open themselves to the youngsters in the name and spirit of Christ. There is no awesome institutional plan or wordy guidelines, except those spelled out in the Bible. There's just a group of compassionate people, opening their lives to a bunch of tattered kids.

Chuck and his people have experienced rejection and failure. Some of the kids they have worked with have gone back to jail, and some of those youngsters have rejected and turned off Chuck's Outreach. But that doesn't faze Chuck and company. They understand the fundamental risk of Christian openness: We may be rejected; then the only company we'll have will be Jesus, who came to His own, opened Himself to His own, and was rejected by His own.

2

THE RISK OF PRESENCE

Complete openness to God, self, and others won't work in solitary confinement. For this reason, the disciple of Jesus has to take the risks of being present in the world. He can't allow himself the luxury of dabbling at the edge of the water. The Jesus-follower has to hold his nose, close his eyes, and plunge in.

Malcolm Muggeridge, the British wit and scholar, was deeply impressed by a group of Scottish monks with whom he spent time while filming a documentary for the BBC. Muggeridge noted that the monks were a sight happier in their poverty than all the frustrated, bickering children of the affluent.

I was telling that story in a church a quarter of a mile from one of the South's largest steel mills. After I had finished, I was going though the handshaking routine when I suddenly felt my hand gripped by a huge frying pan of a hand, the skin of which felt like sandpaper. It was connected to a powerful body, crowned by a face whose scraggly lines and sunset coloring told me the man who wore it worked near the furnaces where molten ore began its conversion into steel. His wasn't a scholar's voice, but no scholar ever made a better point: "Shucks, anybody could be happy not having to butt heads out in the world."

I knew what he was saying. Christian discipleship bears little peril in a place where everyone loves God. It gets risky in the steamy confines of a steel mill, in the clattering chaos of a newspaper city room, in the sterile surroundings of a concrete-and-glass office building, or in the checkout line of a grocery store where prices have rocketed through the ceiling. Jesus' prayer of presence applies to those places as much as it did to the marketplace of old Jerusalem. For He had all His disciples—including those in the twentieth century—in mind when He prayed:

> I pray thee, not to take them out of the world, but to keep them from the evil one. . . . As thou hast sent me into the world, I have sent them into the world. . . .
>
> John 17:15–19 NEB

The point is this: God has chosen ragamuffin people to spread the word that there is reconciliation between God and man and between men. The only way that light shines is for those bearing God's torch to collide with the ponderous darkness of the world. Those who risk being present are the ones who split the night!

One trip to India did more to make me realize this than a year of lectures. I was traveling with John Haggai, the hustling missionary-evangelist on whom the sun seldom sets. John had asked me to make the trip to India with him, and I had immediately envisioned the India of the movies of the forties and fifties, resplendent with mansions, turbaned mystics, and Taj Mahals.

We journeyed all night, skipping across the southern toe —Madras, Madurai, and finally Trivandrum. There we were met by an ivory-frocked priest of the Martoma church, and he drove us deep into the jungle, to the Indian Martoma version of a camp meeting. Thousands of Indian Christians had gathered for days of preaching and singing. The first night, I took to my bunk early, and listened to the strange hymns blaring from the giant arbor where the Jesus people were sitting. It was all alien to me, as if I had been on another planet—everything, that is, except the spirit of the people. Had I not been a Christian, they would have evangelized me without speaking a word, so forceful was the witness of their compassion.

But I was acutely aware of my limitations, especially when I tried to say something about the faith, from my then Washington-based frame of reference. They had made me very much at home, yet I knew I was a stranger to their needs. But what a difference when the Martoma bishop spoke! I could look at the eyes of his listeners and know that this was a man who was touching them where they were. The bishop had been there through the famines which had robbed the people of their children and old ones. He knew the hellish squall of the monsoon, and the threat it bore to their flimsy huts. The bishop had felt the pang of political tension that gripped his people.

It was clear in the green depths of that jungle that, when it comes to ministry, there's no substitute for raw, risky presence! A man can be heard from afar; but he can lead and comfort and be prophetic when he has risked the brotherhood of presence. When he has supped at the table of tragedy with his people, worn the crepe and the wedding crown with them, his people know it. No, there's no substitute for presence, and few risks greater.

This must have been on Dietrich Bonhoeffer's mind when the noose was being readied for the men of Christ in the

Germany of 1939. Some American friends had arranged a lecture tour in their country for Bonhoeffer. He arrived in the United States planning to stay a year, but couldn't squelch the tremor within himself because he was absent from his brothers and their crises.

"Only a fortnight since I left Berlin, and already so much longing for my work," he wrote in a letter on June 16, 1939 (all quotes from Bonhoeffer letters are from Mary Bosanquet in *The Life and Death of Dietrich Bonhoeffer*). And on June 18: ". . . Through my intention and interior necessity, continually to remember the brothers over there and their work, I have been almost abandoning my task over here. . . ."

On June 26, Bonhoeffer read Paul's request to Timothy to "come before winter" (2 Timothy 4), and the words sang across his mind like a summoning bugle. He wrote:

> . . . It is for us as it is for soldiers, who come home on leave from the front, but who, in spite of all their expectations, long to be back at the front again. We cannot get away from it any more. Not because we are necessary, or because we are useful . . . but simply because that is where our life is, and because we leave our life behind, destroy it, if we cannot be in the midst of it again. . . .

So Bonhoeffer went home to Germany, and halfway through the next decade he was swinging at the end of some Nazi hangman's rope.

Presence is a risky business and perhaps that is the reason for the rise in the popularity of isolationism. This tendency seems to be on the ascendance everywhere.

One Sunday morning in New York City, I left Dr. Peale's gleaming church and strolled up Broadway. It was pleasant.

The streets were as bare as if some movie company had emptied them to film the story of the last man on earth. I realized I had never really seen the skyscrapers until I had seen them in silence. But the peace was shattered by a scream of fury half a block away. I hurried in the direction of the scream, and found an old woman standing on a corner. I listened to her cries as they formed a requiem of loneliness. No one cared, she said. There was nothing to go home to, no one to hear, or to be spoken to. She was isolated in an overcrowded world, and isolated because others chose to isolate themselves from her.

A few years earlier in the same city the Genovese girl was standing on the edge of a mob and was murdered in the sight of the mob because they chose the ease of isolation.

A paradox is aborning in the realigning social patterns of America. We are increasingly urbanized, more compact. Spatial distances between people have been altered radically. But we were better friends when we were in the country, living five miles apart. Now we live in great concrete-and-glass structures, sharing corridors, but never seeing one another. There is a door for the butler, one for the service-man, one for the postman, and one for the garbage man. But there is no door for the neighbor. We no longer read about the lonely crowd; we *are* the lonely crowd.

As we become isolationist on a personal level, we do the same on the political level. Again, the paradox is at work. The world shrinks as communications and travel cease to be impediments. Theodore von Laue says that through "global confluence" we perceive the "global city." But empires on which once the sun never set withdraw to tiny islands which have to expend all their resources just to keep afloat. The United States passes through the pall of Indochina and on emerging shakily from the other side is begged to consider the delights of isolationism.

Nor is the church exempt from the isolationist passion. American institutional religion, for the most part, is wedged between two poles. The intensive social revolution of the last decade left many churches foundering on a sea of uncertainty. At last some, driven to hysteria by charges of irrelevance, chose to become neo-humanist institutions, forgetting that with social action there must accompany the ministry of the Spirit.

But others went to the other pole. They became isolated from the world and its agony. Theirs was seen as the business of heaven and in their economy, the business of heaven could have no relationship to the business of living on earth. Such churches became monasteries of sorts, locking their members into mental and spiritual solitude. They, as their sisters on the opposite end of the spectrum, never dreamed there might be a connection between evangelism and social presence.

The funny thing was that often the churches most aggressive on the foreign mission front were those most isolationist on the domestic front. Send doctors and social scientists to Nigeria, but for heaven sake keep them out of the home territory. Set up a coffeehouse in Hong Kong, but eschew all appearances of communication with the coffeehouse crowd in the church neighborhood. Tutor blacks in Rhodesia, but keep your distance locally. Such were the philosophies of the isolationists.

Many had found that doing good was not a bad thing, if it could be done by long distance. The church in isolation thus developed a corps of long-distance good doers, people whose salaries could be paid as surrogate servants. The sin was not in paying servants. The sin was in assuming they were surrogates.

The surrogate corps was absolutely essential for churches who discovered that presence is risky, and who never got the point of incarnation.

The most intimate level of this alien existence is spiritual isolation. Through spiritual isolation, a person lets himself remain separated from God, who is the source of wholeness and purpose for his life. When a man isolates himself from God, he isolates himself from other people, in the deepest sense.

How well I know!

Man lives in a spiritual labyrinth. The corridors are shiny and lonely. There are many other corridors, and many other men. But each lives in his own corridor, and there is no other man with whom the secrets of one's own corridor can be shared. Somehow we men of the labyrinth sense that if there are other beings trapped in the labyrinth, then perhaps there is at least One who can indeed share the terror of our own lonely treks through the corridor.

We organize posses and send them out looking for the One capable of that most intimate presence. We employ prophets and scribes, mystics and magicians and implore, cajole, and harass them to find Him. The calamity of the search is that we finite, incomplete creatures invariably label other finite, incomplete creatures as infinite and whole, and in the end are crushed in disappointment, usually to the extent of death. In that moment, we bow to demonic frustration and cast our outmaneuvered hope on the strained backs of our own value systems, upon other people, and upon our own meager struggle as a race.

Least of all do we expect to find Him present on a barren mountain looming dejectedly on a peninsular desert. But there goes Moses, an ambassador for us all, daring to gaze into the flame of the bush that would not be consumed, in hopes of discovering Presence. The scenario of Exodus 3 tumbles across history and comes out to us like this:

THE VOICE I have heard the anguish of the children of Israel. I have seen the oppression with which the Egyptians crush them. Come now Moses, and I will send you to Pharaoh, and you will be charged with bringing my Israel-child out of Egypt.

MOSES Who am I that I should go before Pharaoh? Who am I that I should lead Israel out of Egypt?

THE VOICE Certainly I will be with you. . . .

MOSES But when I come to the nation of Israel, I shall say to them, "The God of our fathers has sent me to you." And they will want to know, "What is His name?" What then shall I say to them?

THE VOICE I Am that Who I Am. When you address Israel, tell them I Am sent you. . . .

Some would have thought He would have answered: "I am the Universe." Or perhaps, "I am the Ultimate Substance of all things." But when the cliché and the liturgy and the expected are stripped away and Moses asks the name under which he is to execute the command of holiness, a proper noun doesn't do for a name. God identifies Himself as dynamic. His name is a present-tense verb of being present: I Am.

This is that eternally present God who says to contemporary man, "I am not *deus ex machina.*" God's assertion of present being to Moses—and to us—is, in effect, the statement that God is not contingent on the tragedy or victory of Israel for His real being. The "I Am God," in this ancient answer, says to modern man that His being present is not dependent for its reality on those shaky prayers that worm out of frightened mouths as Boeing 707s climb to thirty thousand feet. The "I Am God" is not dependent, for His being present, on civic-club religion, through which His presence is summoned because the program states that the Reverend Smithby will invoke upon God just between the welcome and the mashed potatoes. Such events often signal that God's presence has been ignored as if He were indeed dead and the only reason for prayer is that it is a fine old tradition now extinct from our schools and the least we can do is utter one in foxholes, on Boeing 707s, and at Lions Club meetings.

Such rituals stem from a massive conceit in the human fiber that holds—usually subconsciously—that God's reality, His presence, hovers between poles of the human situation, and is not "there" until summoned from this exile of nonreality by some poor soul up against an impossible wall. God as *deus ex machina* is an elementary concept, and Albert Outler totals it well in *Who Trusts in God* when he says: "Even in the ruckus about the 'death of God' it turned out that what was really at stake was not so much the death of *God* as a burial of the *deus ex machina*— a job that some of us thought had been attended to a century and a half ago."

Still, there is a sense of sadness that enshrouds the Moses experience on Sinai. True, he had the thrill of meeting God face-to-face, and he had the exhilaration of hearing the voice of God give him a sweeping order. But poor Moses didn't get to meet the incarnate God.

To be sprinkled out in a bush is one thing. But to be fleshed out as a man—that is another. The God in the bush was only partly revealed. The God in the man named Jesus is so fully present as to be fully revealed. He no longer hides in a bush. In Jesus, He walks among us. There is no other time in history when God establishes His presence so clearly and so eternally as when He lays it out in Christ.

God comes in Christ and pitches His tent (tabernacles) with us; He comes to His own and His own receive Him not —and no wonder. The pseudodeity we worship before we meet this One so thoroughly present in Christ, is a handy tool, as easily dismissed as He is summoned. That nonincarnate God is our opium, our Freudian projection. He is our garbage disposal, dishwasher, and electric garage door—a button to be pushed, a whim to be exercised. That false god is our rationale at income tax evasion time. It is His will that is said to justify discrimination, bad theology, and a host of other sins begging divine sanction, even if it's counterfeit.

But the really present God—that One who tabernacles with us—gives and commands, and because of that is rejected. But to those who receive His presence, He is really there, and He gives them the power to become the sons of God.

The radical incarnate presence of God in Jesus comes like a cataclysmic earthquake on the seismograph of history. It disturbs the straightness of the line. But we see that coming gives the line dimension, order, purpose. And history will not let us forget how intensely He has been present as the Christ. The Caesars carefully arranged their deity, only to wind up forgotten while a carpenter in a desolate nation is remembered, worshiped, and followed across the generations. Napoleon, perhaps in frustration, said, "This man vanished for eighteen hundred years still holds the characters of men as in a vise." And Phillips Brooks, the Boston preacher, much later was still moved by this radical presence when he said:

> I am far within the mark when I say that all the armies that ever marched, and all the navies that were ever built, and all the parliaments that ever sat, and all the kings that ever reigned, put together have not affected the life of man upon this earth as has that One Solitary Life.

Nowadays, of course, the Life is wrapped in organdy and incense. It is played and replayed like a cassette in plastic buildings chilly with air conditioning and slumberful with padded pews. It is forgotten that the Life was lived midst savage oppression, always on the edge of starvation, carried about daily on feet scorched with dust, and encased in a body that had no roof under which to rest.

Most of all it is forgotten that it was a Life constantly risking itself because it was so radically present. There has been no life for which Blake's words were more true:

> My mother groan'd! my father wept.
> Into the dangerous world I leapt.

It was a world that would hear Him, cheer Him, and spear Him.

What was it about this Life that cost Jesus so much? Why was it that of all beings, the Life of God incarnate was baptized in such constant risk simply because it was *there?* To be sure, there was the physical risk of discomfort that would come to any man living in the destitution of first-century Palestine. There was the ever-present risk of a wrong word, a wrong signal in the presence of the Roman conqueror. That Jesus faced at the hands His tempters. But there were risks far more subtle than those, and it is these subtle risks of presence and the way Jesus handled them that have for us immediate implication and meaning.

To be present in the world as the Christ—or as His body as Paul sees—is to risk being known. How simple a matter is a life buried in the secrecy of isolation. How utterly safe anonymity. No one scorns or rejects the nonpresent, unknown one. Howard Hughes took the glare of being known in his early and middle days and discovered that the best way to live out the last days is through the retreat into isolated mystery. The subpoena servers can't reach him and the questioning reporters can't bug him.

I was in Hong Kong for the first time, and a friend wanted to give me a glimpse of China. We got a car and curled up through the New Territories to a slight promontory at a place called Lak Ma Chau. I gazed down through no-man's-land at a farmer on a collective farm, up to his knees in rice water. In the distance was a barren steppe, punctuated by a ragged mountain range. I derived enough mystery out of the visit to last a year.

Coming back down my friend, a sometime student of Mao (though not a Maoist), began to talk.

"Mao will not die," he said.

"Say that again," I responded.

"Mao will not die as far as the people of China are concerned. They will be told he has gone up into the mountain, and will continue to hand down his teachings from his eternal hermitage."

I mused on the nature of living Mao, everywhere present but nowhere present. He discovered what most earthly despots have found: one rules better when one is not fully known. "Holiness" is linked with mystery, as Paul Tillich would put it. In a democracy, the leader has to let himself be known—or at least be seen—so he can continue to be leader. In a despotic country like China the ruler continues to be leader because he is unknown. Power erodes when the powerful show signs of decay. The competitors smell the blood. Better to hide in the wilderness by a lake when alive, and in the mountains when dead.

Peter and James and John tried to get Jesus to stay up in the mountains once. They had climbed up the mount with Him, not knowing why. When Moses and the angels had finished their visitation with Jesus, the disciples decided it was time to erect a place of worship that doubtless would have become a motel-shrine, complete with a five-and-dime store for the sale of relics. But the Jesus who was God present knew the mountain meant absence. That was the reverse of all He had come to be and do. No wonder He rebuked them.

The ministry of Jesus was always in the form of an intimate presence. His work started with intimate friendships, and in His periods of solitude—which were forced on Him because of the intensity of His presence—He was never far from the disciples. He was always *there*—and when He was not, they crumbled as a unit.

The intimacy of His presence showed that He could stand being known. His presence was of such power that even in the moments when His feet stumbled and the resonance went out of His voice because of thirst and when He wept out of agony, He was still their leader. In fact, it was in those moments when the truth of Himself became best known that He was best able to lead—as when, after that burning moment at Caesarea Philippi He heard Peter say, "Thou art the Christ . . ." (Matthew 16:16 KJV).

We keep on saying it, even after two thousand years, and knowing what we know: that He was destined to die humiliated on a cross. Why do we keep uttering Peter's confession? For the simple reason that the Present One continues to let Himself be known.

It was the Easter after the assassination of Dr. Martin Luther King. I had gone to the copydesk to put my column on the table. Dick stopped me. We kidded often, and sometimes it broke down into serious debate. He said he was an atheist.

"Dr. King lies over in Atlanta buried in a tomb," said Dick. "What if his followers come tonight and spirit away his body, then send some people out there in the morning to discover the empty tomb?" he wondered. "I'll bet that it'd go around the world, and two thousand years from now, you'd have a new religion, built around a new resurrected lord. How do you know that's not how Christianity got started?"

Dick's question burned. Ten pairs of eyes turned on me. I thought the wire machine had stopped clattering. What would I say?

All I knew: "Because, because . . . I know Him."

After all these centuries, He still risks letting Himself be known. This is what Sir Arthur Eddington must have felt when, in a lecture quoted in John Baillie's *Our Knowledge of God,* he said:

> In the case of our human friends we take their existence for granted, not caring whether it is proven or not. Our relationship is such that we could read philosophical argu-

ments designed to prove the non-existence of each other, and perhaps even be convinced by them—and then laugh together over so odd a conclusion. I think it is something of the same kind of security we should seek in our relationship with God. The most flawless proof of the existence of God is no substitute for it; and if we have that relationship the most convincing disproof is turned harmlessly aside. If I may say it with reverence, the soul and God laugh together over so odd a conclusion.

In chapter one, we detailed the *way* in which God, through Christ, lets Himself be known. He identifies His presence with us so clearly, it is mind-boggling to think of the church as having difficulty in screwing up the courage to clearly identify its presence in the world (and here again, we're talking about that individual disciple, who is a "church").

Findley Edge notes that different brains have different notions about what "Christian presence" really is. There are at least four, says Edge, in *The Greening of the Church*. For some, Christian presence means to be present, aware of, and sensitive to social need, but also to be present for verbal witness. For others, it is to be present, again with sensitivity to social problems, but also to assert, in a universalist theology, that the individual *is* saved, irrespective of any commitment to Christ. A third group believes all that is needed is presence, no verbal witness, just "being there." A final school of thought about "Christian presence" is that the Christ-follower must be present to the structures of society, interpreting evangelism as that by which the *structures* are redeemed.

So where do we settle? The Christian—the church—if he

is behaving like his Master, must be present in the world. That much is very clear. And if he is that open person we talked about in chapter one, he is going to be sensitive to the needs of people in society, as well as individually. But because his openness is complete, his presence is going to be complete. That is, he's not going to stand around like a timid nanny. He's going to be compelled by his open compassion to make the big identification and announcement: "I am a follower of Jesus Christ, and I am present to let you know that God wants something to do with you!"

This bold and clearly marked presence was the kind practiced by some friends of mine a while back. They decided they wanted to *do* God's love toward people, and began looking for a vehicle that would provide for some deep opportunities for presence. They decided to start teaching people to read, using the Laubach Method. This meant that each of my friends would spend one night a week with one person for one solid year! Invariably, in the course of study, the person being taught was compelled to ask eventually, "Why in the world are you doing this?" and were my friends ever ready to tell them! The distinction was that they were present, not merely as literacy teachers, but as followers of Jesus Christ. They were literacy teachers, plus!

Jesus has also shown us so clearly that to be present in the world is to risk being identified with certain types of people —like the guilty.

We religious folk often assume we're identifying with the guilty when we go to jails and preach down to convicts from lofty pulpits. And well we should, for Jesus spells it out: "Inasmuch as ye have done it unto one of the least of these my brethren, ye have done it unto me" (Matthew 25:40 KJV). But our preaching would be infinitely more effective if we would take the risk and go to those places where they live *before* they wind up in a cell.

The guilty, of course, are not only those in prison. They are the people society has judged to be "less worthy," people like the insane, practicers of dubious vocations. Sometimes the risk is greater identifying with these guilty ones than with those guilty ones in prison. We go into prison and everyone beholds our mercy. But approval is not so readily available when we go to the back rooms where the political deals are made, to the streets where prostitutes hook their victims.

The incarnate Jesus had this knack for winding up with the guilty. His chances of being crucified would have been reduced had He stuck more closely to those judged by society as the "innocent" and "worthy." But even in His moment of death, He tied up with the thief and let all know that identification with the guilty extends even to the moment of greatest personal crisis. And Carlyle Marney wrote in *He Became Like Us:*

> We could have accepted his identification with his mother or with that disciple who had such capacity for redemption. But here he identifies with our bottom exhibit. . . .

Identification through presence with the guilty is risky because the identifier often comes out looking as guilty as his associate. Sometimes we in Christendom rationalize away this kind of identification by saying that it dilutes our witness. But I can't get out of my mind the fact that this was what Calvary was all about. Jesus came into the world guiltless, got mixed up with my crowd—the guilty—and in the end He was the guy with peanut butter on His face. The powers-that-were tried and punished Him for my guilt, simply because He associated with me!

To be present in Christ's way is to take the risk of identifying with community. The Christian experience is not something that happens in a vacuum of human relationships. Emil Brunner, in his *God and Man,* said that "One cannot get God as Father without at once getting men as one's brothers." Martin Luther was so impressed with the "togetherness" aspect of being a Christian that he toyed with substituting for the word *church,* the word *Gemeinde*—community.

Gurus can retreat to bleak mountains and Buddhas reside under waterfalls, but being a Christian means being related to other people in a community way. "He that loveth not knoweth not God . . .," we read in 1 John 4:8 KJV and, in verse 12, "If we love one another, God dwelleth in us. . . ."

(margin note: no less than 100%)

The community of faith is different from that secular community in which the Christian also lives. In fact, he is present in the community of faith to get charged up for his presence in the secular community. But the difference is in the dynamic. Karl Barth would have been uncomfortable with Luther's *Gemeinde* because to him it would have meant basically a static thing. "What is decisive," said Barth in *God Here and Now,* "is that we learn again to think when we use the word 'Church' not only of an organization, and when we use the better word, 'community' not only of the existence and the condition of a society, but with both words, rather on the event of a gathering." The "event" of the congregating of the community of faith is what makes it the community of faith.

But the "event" is not a wedding, or a funeral, or a confirmation, though these may be part of it. The "event" is the call of God to a particular people, *for mission.*

To be present in the community of Christ is to be in a familylike community. Here's where the risk gets sticky. The pain of another member of my family-community becomes my pain. My risk of being hurt is multiplied by the number of "brothers and sisters."

Churches divide over what kind of government they should use to administer their affairs. But whether it is a hierarchical structure in the style of the Roman Catholics, or a "democracy" *à la* the Baptists, the church must be a theocracy. This means that the members of the community must listen to one another. If God speaks through fishermen and tax collectors and prostitutes, he can speak through anybody in the community of faith!

If presence within one's own family-community is risky, then presence in the world is downright perilous. But, to say it again, the community of faith exists for people on a mission, and their mission is to infiltrate the world. Infiltrators get caught and killed, and sometimes they get labeled, emerging with nasty images.

But without those risks, the presence of the Christian in the world is no more redemptive than that of an alley cat!

3

THE RISK OF IMAGE

"Everybody on Times Square has an angle." He was a cop, and I was accompanying him on his graveyard beat, which covered an area hard by the glittering man-made Milky Way.

I chuckled at his remark, catching the most immediate point. The nature of the place was a lie, designed for seduction. Man had paved its open places, hung the lights which were the stars of the Times Square cosmos. And for what? To make a buck. To rendezvous, and by means of the well-honed lie, make out. To gain momentary glory, buoyed into self-deception by the craft of image, everywhere leaping from the Times Square glimmer.

Back in my stuffy hotel room at 4:00 A.M., I thought some more about what the policeman had said. Survival in Times Square seemed in exact proportion to the artfulness of the deception, the angle. One harvested as one sowed. A good lie meant a good return. But were the Times Square mobs, in their essence, all that different from anyone else? Certainly the devilish schemes ranging from pimping to peddling narcotics weren't universal practices. But the "angles," the magnificent grandstanding to keep everyone from finding out the truth—that behind the facade of gaiety and

glamour, there was an awful lot of sadness and ugliness—
wasn't this a near-univiersal practice? And didn't it all come
down to the protection of image in an age overwrought by
imagery?

What does the Christian do in the Times Square world?
It bothered me. I knew that even as a follower of Jesus, a
majority of my contemporaries and I were in the image-
protecting business. One of the hardest things for us to risk
was our image.

So what the cop really meant was that everybody on
Times Square has an image to protect. We don't all live on
Times Square, but we do find ourselves neighbors in a curious age historically, one that Marshall McLuhan, the media
philosopher, has called the "iconic age." Whatever else the
iconic age may mean, it certainly signifies an era in which
man has apparently concluded that he can no longer function in public on the basis of what he really is. For what he
has been conditioned to think his essential being to be is
image, nothing more than cloudy image. Life's meaning in
the iconic age is to sort through all the image options until
one that satisfies is found. After it has been worn for a while,
the wearer usually announces he has "found himself." Protecting one's image against the horrid onslaught of what-
really-is requires the most artful dodge, the master angle.

The iconic age is terribly intense. Thousands of times each
day, potential consumers are slapped in the face with new
images to buy. Since there is usually some material item
which is being hawked, we aren't always aware that what
they're really trying to sell us is image. Thus the iconic age
is marked by subtlety, and the Christian who is called to risk
his image is sometimes duped by the subtlety, to the extent
that he doesn't realize that he's failing to lay his image on

the altars of the iconic age. The temptation to cling to image in the shrewd, tough (also images) iconic age works heavily on the Christ-follower. It usually goes something like this: "Be sure you look as shrewd, tough, swinging (or whatever image happens to be in vogue) as the group to which you're trying to communicate the gospel, or you won't have any credibility." Or, the crafty little line the iconic age hurls at the church reads thusly: "You'd better maintain a good front, or you won't be able to attract all those great numbers of people you're after."

Maybe we can get a better hold on the iconic age by taking a look at its predecessor period. Back then, for example, wooden Indians stood in front of quaint stores holding fistfuls of cigars. No one bothered much about what the Indian meant, except to note that he made one heck of a good cigar holder. Nowadays, we are supposed to get as excited about the Indian as the cigar. The iconic age has conditioned us to think that maybe we will get the fine traits of the Indian—wisdom, strength, perseverance—if we smoke the cigar. But in the (to us) primeval age prior to the iconic age, they consumed the cigar, not whatever, together, cigar and Indian meant.

Picture and reality usually clash in the iconic age. We citizens of the epoch have learned how to deal with that problem: submerge reality for the sake of the image, the icon. Who cares that that swift little sports car is built like a tin can, and just begs to be crushed by some mammoth truck? People look "cool" when they drive sports cars, and that's what counts (and as the owner of a red matchbox job, I certainly ought to know).

I don't believe they'll make a man in the laboratory, but the iconic age has certainly chiseled out its own kind of

creature. Call him the "iconic consumer." He prefers pur-
chasing image rather than essence. Some commentators say
he lives in a state of perma-war, since he always has to be
popping off his guns somewhere. Maybe so. But he definitely dwells in a state of perma-confusion, like the hero of
Thomas Merton's book *My Argument With the Gestapo:*
"I always understood the landscape in terms of something
else, what the landscape had been once, or what the techni-
cians dreamed it ought to have been." The iconic consumer
would like very much to consume the landscape for itself.
But his frustration is eternal, because he has been taught not
to think of the landscape's reality, but its image. Thus he
sees the landscape in contrast to the way it might look
through a Technicolor camera. Usually, the reality fails to
measure to the image, and the iconic consumer is disap-
pointed. One can't help but wonder if this doesn't have
something to do with the restlessness of modern young
people, who, as children, grew up in front of the magic box
with the cold, blue stare.

The weird thing about all this is that the iconic consumer,
for all his frustration and disappointment, *prefers* it that
way. "The deeper problems connected with advertising
come less from the unscrupulousness of our 'deceivers' than
from our pleasure in being deceived . . ." says Daniel Boor-
stin in *The Image.* The iconic consumer is a masochist of
the spirit, reveling in the sting of the image-lie. He welcomes
it, for he has learned one thing: Image is preferable to reality.

This is doubly true when it comes to Christian witness. So
long as the image of the message comes through with the
accent on the positive—heaven, eternal life, the comforting
presence of Christ—everything is hunky-dory. The risk
comes in preaching that high-risk, low-image stuff. Who's

going to sparkle his teeth on television, telling people about hell, about some of the strenuous demands of Christian discipleship? Communicating the gospel in the iconic age is a complex chore because of the temptation to reduce the risk of failure and slice some of the reality that hurts, for the sake of image.

Something else about this creature called the iconic consumer: The iconic age winds up molding him into a Pavlovian animation, and *presto!* you have the next step on the evolutionary scale, the reiterate consumer. The commodity may not change, but the image certainly does—and in order to possess the new image, the reiterate consumer gobbles up the same old commodity again and again. In the age of the icon, ultimate delirium is that of an advertising account executive who fears his creative people are slipping in introducing exciting new images for staid, old products.

Advertising, of course, writes the lyrics for the music to which the iconic-age consumers dance like marionettes. Scads of modish executives are ensconced in gleaming office towers, feeding off the iconic consumer's fierce insistence that he be lied to. Cigarette advertising has developed a particularly refined art of deception. Anyone who has ever smoked knows that cigarettes feel and taste basically the same. A brand like Marlboro languished in sales under a jingle that urged, "Escape from the commonplace." Cigarettes were, by their nature, commonplace, and that was simply too much a snow job for consumers to hook on to. Then a seventy-year-old advertising man named Leo Burnett got the account, and introduced consumers to the Marlboro man. The thrust of the advertising was the temptation to become the tough, wind-dusted Marlboro man, to escape to "Marlboro country." The cigarette was still the same old conglomeration of tars, nicotine, and wrapping paper, but it had a new image. After that new image had been peddled to the public, Marlboro moved up the sales chart, at last becoming third in the country. Burnett pulled off the same trick for Virginia Slims. In an age when women were having all the drama of the suffrage battle recreated through Women's Lib, Burnett sold his cigarettes with the image-creating jingle, "You've come a long way, baby." Since Virginia Slims were aimed at women consumers, both the motto and the cigarette name were carefully selected for image impact. What woman doesn't want to be "slim"? Of course, many iconic-age consumers missed the point that Burnett's scheme with Virginia Slims (to say nothing of the Marlboro man) was horridly contemptuous. It took what for some women was a serious moral issue and tried to use it as a gimmick to peddle cigarettes.

The temptation of the Christian trying to get across his message in the iconic age is to reduce the gospel to the level of gimmick. To do so makes it only one more competitor among the many vying for the consumer's attention every day. Certainly, we followers of Christ must get with it in trying to win men's attention. But we have to take the risk of presenting the gospel on its own terms, not in the guise of some nifty little attachment to life that makes things feel better. Aspirin is supposed to do that!

One of the deepest tragedies of the iconic age is that it has contributed so thoroughly to the dehumanization of man. The peculiar vision of the age demands that people be seen in terms of the kinds of images they might like to wear, and not in terms of authentic human need. Gradually, the process goes to the root of the consumer's consciousness. He unwittingly comes to regard himself as a puppet-object, and, in the end, reduces his fellows to the same level. What results is a mutual contempt. Consumers are objectified by advertisers (certainly an act of contempt) and the consumer, knowing at his bottom level that someone is trying to fool him, comes to hold in contempt advertisers, and, ironically, their products.

Take politics. Media elections have become the more blatant examples of dehumanization in the iconic age. Before the 1972 elections, in his syndicated column, Russell Baker took wry note of the problem. Speaking of candidates photographed in pastoral settings, Baker said:

> The assumption of political marketing is that the electorate is such a mass of nincompoops that needing a product to give them 21 per cent fewer wars and abolish taxes all day long, they will go ahead and buy something because they have seen it photographed in the woods looking innocuous.

But the consumer in such a system must inevitably become dehumanizer as well as dehumanized. "The marketers," continued Baker, "may retort that their assumption is right, that the market has bought, and will buy again this year, nothing more promising than lovingly staged live meat." Thus the choice in the media politics of the iconic age becomes one of image-objects (called consumers) deciding between other image-objects (called candidates). Said Baker, "Give the people a choice for Congress: Bill Smith in the woods, or Pan Am making the going great. . . ." (From The New York Times, September 21, 1970.)

Okay. I know all this blather I've worked myself into over advertising sounds a bit hypocritical. I've worked in the newspaper business. My paycheck wouldn't have been possible without advertising. In fact, there's a very good argument that can be made around the thesis that without advertising, a free press wouldn't exist. Someone else—the government—would have to finance the media, and that would be the end of the Fourth Estate. And there is good advertising. It doesn't try to manipulate the consumer with a bill of goods scrawled on nothing but imagery. It doesn't taunt the consumer with the *inadequacy of what he is,* but with the *inadequacy of certain products he may own.*

Since the iconic age plays such a powerful role in shaping our thoughts about ourselves and others, as well as our value systems, there is hardly a greater need than that its hypocrisies be exposed and challenged. The irony is that the hypocrisies of the iconic age are so subtle and so infectious that those who would render the challenge of themselves become icons, existing after a while more on image than substance. The New Left and the counterculture were supposed to challenge our "dishonesty." Then hair and flared trousers took up residence in the J.C. Penney catalog, looking as stylish there as on the body of a young revolutionary. The prerequisite to marching against capitalism on Pennsylvania Avenue became a visit to the boutiques of Georgetown for purchase of the uniform. Who is there to take the risks of shattering the icon—no, the idol—of imagery by which we have come to live and breathe? Who has the courage to call the shots as they are, not to wear the actor's mask?

The disciples of Jesus ought to be scrambling to volunteer for that mission, because no one has dealt with icons so boldly as Christ! Every breath taken by the incarnate Christ demanded risk of His image. The very fact of incarnation—

meaning that God washes Himself of the image of deity in order to become man—bespeaks risk. The incarnation is a general risk of image. Daily, in that incarnate life, Jesus took the specific risks—the same ones He calls His disciples to take.

Few things etch image for a person more than the crowd he runs with. It was no less true two thousand years ago than now. Jesus, after all, was incarnate in an age when men skirted Samaria to, among other things, avoid the taint to image of being seen with half-breed Samaritans. The world of Jesus of Nazareth was one in which men vied for the best seats at banquets, so they might be seen near the right people.

Had the penchant for image existing in the period of the incarnate Jesus had the nifty public relations and communications skill of our day, some of the results could have been disastrous. What if, for example, there had been a man of great PR savvy among the disciples, and he had had the media available now? Jesus, with His enthralling charisma, might have been portrayed in a contemplative mood out in the wilds near the Sea of Galilee, and a velvet-throated announcer would have said something like, "Follow Jesus, the really good guy." With His powerful personality, Jesus would have had every media agent around tagging after Him. There would have been no place for the multitudes who wanted to get near Him. They would have been blocked by television crews and their cameras, lights, meters, and slick commentators. Someone would be shoving aside the lame and blind to get a light reading. The feeding of the five thousand would have been heralded with a mike check: "Testing, one, two. . . ."

The first thing Jesus' PR man would have faced would

have been the sticky problem of getting rid of the bums who followed Jesus. Announcing that He had come to hang out His shingle for the sick, Jesus collected about Himself the spiritually wheezing, hacking, limping, ninety-seven-pound weaklings. Vernard Eller, in *The Promise,* reminds us that they were known in Hebrew as the *'amme ha-ares.* Once the term, Eller continues, had meant simply, "peoples of the land." Later, the rabbis used the words to denote people not in full compliance with the rituals of the religious observances, and who were weak in their knowledge of the Torah. According to James L. Price in *Interpreting the New Testament,* the Pharisees saw the *'amme ha-ares* as the "violaters of the grave precepts of the Torah, robbers and adulterers, and with 'tax collectors,' that notorious group of apostates, the hated symbols of Jewish subjection to foreign rule."

In another time, the *'amme ha-ares* might have been called *nigger,* or *wop,* or *yid,* or even *WASP.*

Jesus' association with the *'amme ha-ares* drove the religious establishment up the wall. He spelled out their dilemma in Matthew 11:18, 19:

> For John came, neither eating nor drinking, and they say, 'He is possessed.' The Son of Man came eating and drinking, and they say, 'Look at him! a glutton and a drinker, a friend of tax-gatherers and sinners!' And yet God's wisdom is proved right by its results.
>
> NEB

Jesus was relentless in the way He tantalized the ecclesiastical elite. They wanted to know the authority by which Jesus acted, and He replied:

. . . tax-gatherers and prostitutes are entering the kingdom of God ahead of you. For when John came to show you the right way to live, you did not believe him, but the tax-gatherers and prostitutes did; and even when you had seen that, you did not change your minds and believe him.

Matthew 21:31, 32 NEB

And when Jesus selected the band of men who would be His most intimate associates, the people to whom He would give the major roles in beginning the work of changing the world, He chose from among the *'amme ha-ares!* At Caesarea Philippi, He rested His eyes on one of the weakest of these men and said to him, "Blessed art thou, Simon Bar-jona. . . . Upon this rock I will build my church . . ." (Matthew 16:17, 18 KJV). I can almost hear the other apostles twittering and snickering as Jesus said the kind of person Simon was was the prototype of God's Kingdom, and that impetuous, ever-changing Simon would be henceforth known as "Rocky."

Jesus thus lays clear the potential of the church living and speaking His Word, for challenging the icon of association that pollutes human relations in our age. At the same time, His actions castigate image-hungry churches which are mistakenly building cults of Apollo. This quasi-faith teaches by inference that the greatest in the Kingdom of God are beauty queens, sports heroes, and beautiful people in general.

I was saved from organizing a cult of Apollo by a chubby, lisping boy in Texas. We were in a youth retreat, and I had selected for our camp pastor one of the real he-men then lighting the skies of evangelism like great, sizzling comets. One night, after fourteen girls had swooned, the fat kid pulled me aside. "Do you think there's any place in the

Kingdom of God for somebody like me?'' he asked. My concept of communicating the Gospel tumbled in like a strutless tent. Everything about the image-rejecting ministry of Jesus cried out that the Kingdom of God was for the likes of my effeminate, flabby friend!

In the era of the incarnate Jesus, piosity was as cherished a plank in building image as the lack of it is in this day. Perhaps the piosity of that period should be labeled as pseudopiety since it concentrated on peripheral matters and neglected the weightier matters. The "pseudo" applies because the Pharisees and their spiritual companions had the wrong definitions, the wrong priorities for genuine piety. The problem was not that they were not good people. In fairness to them, they were deeply committed to what some of them no doubt believed to be absolute truth. It's just that they were piosity-machines, equipped with a goodness button. The button was pushed in those times when piosity could make the best showing—in teeming marketplaces and crowded synagogues.

So these image experts felt terribly threatened when Jesus came on the scene, in the freedom of true piety, rather than in the restrictiveness of piosity. There was, for example, that day when some starry-eyed believers let a paralytic down through the ceiling of the house where Jesus was ministering. Jesus looked at the board-stiff body and said to the paralytic, "Child, your sins are forgiven you" (see Matthew 9:2). Note the contrast between Jesus and the ecclesiastics, in priorities. The first thing noted by the experts of things theological was that Jesus had had the audacity to say, "Your sins are forgiven you." Never mind that this might be the formula by which a paralytic might walk; it was impious by their measure, even blasphemous. And for anybody else but Jesus, it would have been impious. Jesus took note of the grumbling among the religious elite, and He said to them, in essence: "I wanted you to know that the Son of Man does have power on earth to forgive sins; fellow—get up and walk." The next thing everybody knew, the former paralytic was hoisting his bed over his head!

This makes it a bit surprising that the religious image-merchants just a little later made the same mistake again. Now Jesus was walking on the beach, when He spotted Levi. The man had the misfortune of being a tax collector. A worse turncoat there could not have been. He gathered money from his own people and parceled it back to the Romans as they dictated. He helped keep alive the horrid political machine that sapped the freedom of his own people. He probably would have turned in his own grandmother had she not been prompt in paying her taxes. Even across the centuries, it's still hard to love him! But Jesus, of all things, invited Himself to Levi's house for dinner.

To compound the scandal, there were other tax collectors and assorted disreputable scalawags there. The whole affair was a slap in the face of piosity. The experts in the law took note. Again, Jesus established the priority: "It is not those who are well who need a doctor, but those who are sick" (see Mark 2:17). Jesus had come to cure men of spiritual and physical ills, even if to do so, He might have to risk breaking the contemporary ideas of piosity.

We contemporary disciples must be prepared to risk the image of our piosity if it is necessary in spreading the Gospel. The imperativeness of that risk was underscored for me a while back, during a missions conference in Singapore. I was lecturing on the importance of the Christian communicator being aware of the secular movements that form the thought patterns of his people, and how that communicator would have to risk being seen in the places where sinners reside. A deeply committed Indian Christian disagreed. He argued that it would be wrong to break the mantle of piosity people expect a Christian to wear, and that the tactics I had suggested might be too much of a risk. Suddenly a young Argentine, whose mission territory was the inner city of Buenos Aires, exploded: "How many people have been lost because we were too pious to go to them?"

It's not that the Christian has to adopt modes of impiety. He doesn't join in the practices of adultery and drunkenness in order to "identify." He doesn't have to become a fan of pornography to "understand." He doesn't have to swear to look "relevant," nor swing with ribaldry. But it may be that he has to be present where those kinds of things are going on. There are some sinners who will never come to our churches, and if we're going to snare them, we've got to go where they are. If we do, our images of piosity may be put on the line.

In Jesus, the icon of false piety is rebuked. It sets it up for the sham it is, and in assault after assault, pounds it to shreds, so that image will no longer block awareness to the real. "Do not suppose that I have come to abolish the Law and the prophets," He says. "I did not come to abolish, but to complete" (Matthew 5:17, 18 NEB).

All this means that the church must risk its image of piosity to do God's work. Only then can the church teach the world genuine piety. Let her follow that true piety, and God will take care of the image. What is that true piety? It is seeing people in terms of their spiritual need, and as souls Christ died for, not in terms of how we will look if they worship with us and we minister to them. Not long ago, a denomination announced that a controversial figure would address one of its meetings. One pastor acknowledged that the church, built on the bedrock of faith, had nothing to fear from the character. "But," he added plaintively, "I'm afraid of what it'll do to our image." The church, he was saying, should scuttle truth for the sake of image! He may as well have been preaching that we can forget the idea that wars are won, not by sidestepping the enemy to avoid the bad image of being seen in his presence, but by meeting him head-on.

Maybe Dietrich Bonhoeffer best summed up the way Christ teaches and shows us how to risk our image when he wrote, in *Christ the Center:*

> [Christ] goes incognito as a beggar among beggars, as an outcast among the outcast, despairing among the despairing, dying among the dying. He also goes as sinner among the sinners, yet in that He is *peccator pessimus* (Luther), as sinless among sinners.

But He does not remain incognito, and there is the risk.

As He comes among us—the image-hounds—it becomes clear He is for *us.* For *we* are the image-hounds, the *'amme ha-ares,* the commoners who fear that the reality of themselves is not enough and never will be. But He shows and empowers us to reach beyond image, to the reality of Himself and what we can be in Him. Now we have a new image —that of His slave. But in some wonderful, inexplicable way, because we now have the capacity to live in essence, not in image, we are curiously and marvelously liberated!

4

THE RISK OF BEING POWERLESS

A valiant troop of flowers shouted out their colors at the base of the most perfectly carved stone sphere I had ever seen. The giant globe rested on the grounds of the hacienda in which Costa Rica's President Jose Figueres and his family lived. The rock monolith had been carved by prehistoric Indians who had once occupied the jungles of Central America. President Figueres and I admired the impossbily round stone, and, almost in a whisper, he said, "There is something about man that drives him to try to create monuments to perfection. It is a never-ending quest for beauty and truth."

And power, I thought. Perhaps the Indians had been in a contest with nature, attempting to best her orderly precision, and the Indians had shown some remarkable power. They had been able to move gargantuan chunks of stone, in an age long before mechanical muscles would amplify the paltry strength of men. The Indians had made a mockery of the mathematical challenge of the perfect sphere. They were sensitive artists, but they were people of unusual power, I thought. Not satisfied merely to exercise power over one another, they had taken on natural law, and in looking at the giant stone ball, I had to award the Indians a round.

Man's power-games are as old as the human race. Much of the progress he has made has been an effort to win—to achieve power over other men, over ideas, over the cosmos itself. The struggle has become such a massive one that those who appear short of power, the weak, are held in general contempt, and if not that, at least pity. Survival is the *summum bonum,* and power is the key.

Into such a world comes Jesus of Nazareth, blowing our minds with His shocking disclosure: "The meek shall inherit the earth" (*see* Matthew 5:5). Poppycock! We answer back, smiling knowingly at our arsenals and our textbooks and the museums where we desposit the remnants of our climb up the power ladder. But the authentic disciple of Christ hears, and understands that his Master is calling him to the incredible risk of weakness, of being powerless in a world which gauges everything by power!

more risk today than ever before

Where that world is weak in power, it fakes it. With its art, it molds horrendous masks, and its primitive, rather powerless people don the masks, whistling in the awesome dark of a demonic world. The bold assertion of power is carried in raising the monuments which taunt the heavens. The rhetoric of the trembling, power-seeking world steams in its contrived audacity. The weak had best stand aside, for the powerful, in their desperate dash to nowhere, will arm out any in the way.

But the weak, in the end, will come out on top, says the Christ. Dare we risk meekness? Can the disciples of Christ really buy this line—that the meek will win?

Our experience in the world's crucible teaches us that the weak lose. They get passed off as irrelevant dregs on society. And we forget that the powerful take hefty lumps, and in the end are no more invulnerable than the weak. What about those twenty-one civilizations which have strutted their might across the admiring face of the planet? What about that gangling line of monarchs who, when on the throne, thought themselves the consummation of man's stab at power? We can't even remember most of their names.

What about Adolf Hitler? The man who wrecked the world through a distorted racism and perversion of power gave us all kinds of little hints about his view of power, but we failed to read them.

Albert Speer, Hitler's architect and defense minister, probes deeply into Hitler's troubled psyche in his book *Inside the Third Reich.* In many ways, the book could have been more aptly titled *Inside Hitler.* Speer recounts Hitler's penchant for the monumental. The plotter of the Thousand-Year Reich often remarked that all that was left of "the great epochs of history" were the giant monuments. Hitler thought of the Roman Forum, the scattered carcass of one of the most powerful civilizations. There was the Parthenon, speaking of Greece's Golden Age. Persepolis, Troy, the civilizations of the Incas and the Aztecs seemed to have had their only immortality in stone.

In a chapter he calls "Architectural Megalomania," Speer tells about Hitler's plans for Nuremberg. An elephantine party-rally area would be built, costing $750 million and covering seven square miles. I read the inflated dreams of Adolf Hitler, the world's most frustrated nonartist, and thought of the period when, in the midsixties, I had lived in Nuremberg. On sunny afternoons, my wife and I would sometimes putter over the remains of that dream in our Volkswagen. How ironic it seemed, to drive a beetle-shaped car over the territory where Hitler tried to play messiah, and summoned his people to subdue humanity. The Volks-

wagen and the weed-infested parade grounds were the remnants of Hitler's "power."

Speer tells that in Hitler's retreat near Berchtesgaden in
1940, there was a globe with a pencil line following the
Urals, separating what Hitler envisioned as the spheres of
influence of Germany and Japan. And there was Hitler himself, planning the attack on the Soviet Union. On the eve of
the assault, Hitler could think only of his architectural
megalomania, and told Speer, "We'll be getting our granite
and marble from there, in any quantities we want." Soon
one of the most devastating chapters of World War II—
including the nine-hundred days of Leningrad, the deaths of
legions of soldiers in cold, lonely, snowy traps—would be
written. But the author could think only of a means of symbolizing his power—his monuments!

Maybe if intelligent men of that time had had the fore-
sight to note Hitler's passions for the monumental, they
would have stumbled on the clue that he was a mon-
strously dangerous man. Speer later recalls Aristotle's line:
"It remains true that the greatest injustices proceed from
those who pursue excess, not from those who are driven
by necessity."

In balance, let it be said that a passion for the monumental
need not always symbolize something negative or diaboli-
cal. But even in positive form, the art of the monumental
exists to give man a way of expressing or symbolizing
power. The planners of Washington, D.C., no less than
those of the *Champs Elysée,* or Versailles, or Westminster,
or the Kremlin, were seeking to assert the strength and
stability of their nations when they raised massive buildings
and monuments. On more than one occasion, I have
walked Washington and felt diminished, dwarfed physically

and emotionally by the gray-and-white giants lining the streets.

Even the church has not been exempt from architectural megalomania. Gothic cathedrals, we are told, are granite hymns to God, signifying and confessing His power. Many great churches are built from that motivation. But sometimes the unspoken compulsion is to signify human power. It comes with ministers, insecure in their work, or laymen, insecure in their faith. One pastor I knew became so enamored with the edifice complex, his motivations were unveiled for what they were. Everybody knew why he built the largest sanctuary in his denomination, saddling his people with a debt that virtually prevented mission. Another minister raised a great white elephant of a church sanctuary even before he had educational space to accommodate all the people required to fill the giant hall. Then there was the preacher who advertised his new monument as "the religious showplace of the South." A faith teaching that the meek would inherit the earth seemed strangely out of place there, as did the summons from Christ to risk being weak in a world mad with power. The churches seemed to be saying to the world, "Your power-games are real and right, and we can play it (show it) as skillfully as you!"

Hang on, though. This is not to smirk at all big church buildings, where they are needed, and where they are functional. It is to express concern over turning the great church buildings into means of symbolizing man's power.

For the really powerful people are not those who vent their strength through architectural monuments or diplomatic and strategic prowess, or the ability to hold sway over other people. The really powerful are those who can throw off the temptation to power.

Man's tantalizing fascination with power has intensified

because, Lewis Mumford believes, there has been a revival of the worship of power, not all that different from the periods when spiritual primitives worshiped the sun. In his book *The Pentagon of Power,* Mumford equates the intensification of power hunger with "the return of the sun-god." The sun-god, with the other "sky deities," as Mumford calls them, had their birth in antiquity, when men began to study the heavens in the pursuits of astrology, calendar-making and other sciences and pseudosciences.

Mumford thinks that the technological revolution of the sixteenth century was a religious as well as a scientific phenomenon. In this new age, ". . . the human race counted for little more than an ephemeral swarm of midges on the planet itself. By contrast, science, which had made this shattering discovery by the mere exercise of common human faculties, not divine revelation, became the only trustworthy source of authentic and reputable knowledge."

Ironically, in the pinch to feel power, man sublimated the truth that those facts he discovers in science are revealed because God reveals them. In this sense there was "divine revelation," and, indeed, there would be no scientific discovery without "divine revelation."

For a while in those early days, there was an attempt to keep alive a duality: traditional theological concepts here, the new science there. Eventually, though, the duality collapsed, theology and technology married, and the worship of power, symbolized in the new "suns," was reinstated. Johannes Kepler, the seventeenth-century mystic-scientist, composed the litany of the new power religion:

> . . . lest perchance a blind man deny it to you, of all bodies in the universe the most excellent is the sun, whose essence is nothing less than the purest light, than which there

is no greater star: which single and alone is the producer, conserver, and warmer of all things: it is a fountain of light, rich in fruitful heat and most fair, limpid, and pure to the sight, the source of vision, portrayer of all colours, though himself empty of colour, called king of the planets for his motion, heart of the world for his power, its eye for his beauty, and which alone we should judge worthy of the Most High God, should he be pleased with a material domicile and choose a place in which to dwell with the blessed angels.

Kepler may not have intended it, but what he rendered was an apotheosis of the sun.

It may well be that Mumford has stretched here and there to make a point, that some of his conclusions about the worship of power are too extreme. But it is clear that the quest for power has become an activity that reaches to the deepest levels of man's spirit, and if one accepts Paul Tillich's definition of religion as a quest for ultimates, then humanity's grab for power has a stark religious stripe about it.

One characteristic of religious quest is compulsion. Man finds himself compelled to this or that, and it is a religious quest. Inevitably, he searches for ultimate values and truths. He claims on occasion to be an atheist, but can't get around the drive to enthrone something as the god of his life. Since, as observed earlier, power seems the most expeditious route to survival, the effort to accumulate it becomes one of life's inevitables. We learn as well that the powerful often get the edge on the search for truth and the other inevitables, since they are able to spend time on something other than naked survival.

The fact that this kind of power is usually available only to a few is what forces some people to loathe power and its possessors.

Ellen and Mike (fictitious names for two very real people) were about as naïve to the inevitability of the power-religion as any two people I have ever met. They were college students who had come all the way to Washington from the West, to protest what they sincerely regarded as a misappropriation of power by the United States in Vietnam. They had come for the May Day demonstrations of 1971. It was to have been a tour de force of "people power." Around the land, to the campuses, cliques, claques, communes, and carrels, the summons had been sounded: "We will go to Washington in May, and we will shut down the wicked instrument of slaughter and aggression which is the American government; we will deprive the powerful of their power, and we, the people, will take up the mantle."

For someone who writes books about risk, I did a curious thing: I carefully laid plans to avoid the May Day people. I would wait until the police had cleared the streets, then I would steal in from the Virginia suburbs, bolt across the Roosevelt Bridge, and into the safety of my well-guarded office building.

But Ellen and Mike, gratefully, were not going to give me such an easy cop-out. Early in the afternoon of May Day eve, I was visiting in the office of a senator. Ellen and Mike were there to visit with the senator also, and we wound up in the same waiting area. Gradually, we were drawn into conversation. It moved from banality to cordiality to the spilling of the biggest sop of disillusionment I had encountered.

They were true believers, and had come to Washington

to make a genuine stand for peace. They had wearied of the power-game. They wanted to come together with people with no passion for personal power. They could not resist the trumpet calling them to Washington and May Day.

But Ellen and Mike had not even had time to roll out their sleeping bags at May Day camp before they were being sucked into a seething internal power play developing among the May Day leaders. One group, Ellen and Mike told me, was determined to wrest the major role from the May Day "establishment" (the rawest of irony is that those who wish to destroy establishments become establishments to do so). The two kids moved from group to group, listening to the plotting. At one point, Ellen got fed up with it all and dissented. The May Day power structure put spies on her tracks the rest of the day.

Now Ellen and Mike sat in a senator's office telling the man from Uncle (Sam) that they still wanted to make their statement for peace, but how crushed they were that even in the counterculture they were unable to escape power-games.

I wanted to tell them that they had simply gone to the wrong place to escape the power-game, that the escape was here, or there. But I could not think of an institution or group devoid of power politics. The best I could do—and this would have been the best under any circumstances—was to tell them that power plays are inevitable, and that the task of the Christian in such a milieu is to try, by the power of God, to prevent the usage of power from becoming distorted and immoral. I have an idea that Thucydides understood this power determinism. In one of his plays he has an Athenian general pleading for the surrender of Melos say:

> Of the gods we believe and of men we know that a neces-
> sary law of their nature they rule wherever they can. . . .
> Right, as the world goes, is only in question between equals
> in power, while the strong do what they can and the weak
> suffer what they must. . . .

In world politics, the maxim for survival is the balance of
power. The five power centers, according to the Nixon-
Kissinger definition—the United States, the Soviet Union,
the People's Republic of China, Western Europe, and Japan
—call the shots (a horribly apt analogy). The rest of the
world is reduced to being "client states," shaping their
policy in the image of whatever power they look to for
protection. In a House of Commons debate in 1955, Winston Churchill described eloquently the kind of world the
worship of the sun-god has led us to create:

> Then it may well be that we shall, by a process of sublime
> irony, have reached a stage in this story where safety will
> be the sturdy child of terror, and survival the twin brother
> of annihilation.

Sir Winston is dead, but we got to that "stage in this story"
before they had broken ground for his grave!

For all the impact it has on our lives, though, most of us
have little to do with the global power-game. Our power
struggles are on a much more immediate and basic level.
But this level does have very strong bearing on global politics. The world-scale and national power struggles are probably little more in character than geometric expansions of
the power-games we learn in the parent-child, husband-
wife, sibling-sibling, and neighbor-neighbor power-games.

We talk, for example, a great deal about the "gaps" that exist between various cross sections of humanity. For the most part, these are microcosmic wars fought to see who gets power over whom.

One of these wars has been labeled the "generation gap." Often, the battles are fought around the problem of people of different ages trying to communicate with one another on sensitive issues. But it is deeper than that. It is a power struggle of the first magnitude. For, more than anything else, the generation gap seems to be the failure of parents and children to realize a proper balancing of powers in their relationships. The formula for balancing the equation of power-relationships between parent and child (the most immediate participants in the generation gap) is given in Ephesians 6:1,4:

> Children, obey your parents, for it is right that you should. . . . You fathers, again, must not goad your children to resentment, but give them the instruction, and the correction, which belong to a Christian upbringing.

NEB

Children being obedient to their parents are people who have surrendered a measure of power. Parents stifling their pettiness so as not to "goad" their children to resentment, are hedging their power. For a generation gap occurs when a parent tries to become overly ambitious in the exercise of his power over the child. A generation gap is also the result when a child seeks to free himself totally of any power exerted by the parent, and, in this negative way, exert power over the parent.

Charlie Shedd, in his book *Promises to Peter,* says that his family "credo" for parent-child relationships goes like this:

> The more sensible self-government we allow at the right
> time, the better things will be all the time—better for the
> children—better for us—better for their future—better for
> ours.

This is an excellent starting point. It recognizes the power
of the parent (and indeed, the responsibility) to recognize
and grant self-government in the youngster, thereby
conceding the right of the child to have a shot at governing
himself.

Sometimes, of course, the generation gap happens as
the result of a malicious chain reaction, in which the parents, through their experiences as children, have known
no other style of life, and pass it down to their kids with
raven hair and brown eyes. In these cases, there was a gap
long before the children entered the scene. It was the marriage gap, which pitted two people against one another in
a battle for the emergence of the most powerful. There is
no more apt piece of art to symbolize this kind of relationship than the sculpture of the man and woman locked in
combat and titled *The Eternal Struggle.* Sometimes the
struggle winds up in a court, and the judge plays Caesar,
deciding whether or not to give the thumbs down to one
of the combatants.

In this type of marriage, the battle, as a rule, can't be
ended until one side or the other wins, and then the halt is
often only for resupply. Keith Miller, author of *A Taste of
New Wine,* pins down a basic point of marital conflict
when he talks about the need of partners remaking one
another to suit the image they have sculpted for the spouse:

> So what do we have?—*two* creators, *two gods,* in the soul
> of one marriage . . . each vying, each insisting on the

validity of his own created image of what a husband and wife, what a marriage ought to be.

yes! yes!
yes!

That nasty little matter of winning can become the most sinister demon ripping at the soul of a marriage. It is sometimes the force which drives a man into adultery—he has to prove he's not owned, bossed, or controlled by his wife. Winning is sometimes the force which spurs a woman to uncontrolled spending, to the bleak hopelessness that part of her personhood is being denied. Eventually, lucky couples discover that conflicts between them never come to a truce until one or the other gets ego off center stage and decides he or she doesn't have to win. That requires a lot of willingness to risk, especially when the "vanquished" was unequivocally right to begin with, and knows it!

In sorting through some of the power struggles that corrupt and complicate our relationships on the most immediate level, we inevitably come to the problem of race relations. The race issue, to a large extent, is related to the balancing of powers between people. It is true that some black and white people don't like one another simply because they are black or white. In that sentence, you could substitute all kinds of things for "black and white"—Indians and whites, Chinese and Malays, Chicanos, Flemish, and so on until every race on earth has been cataloged.

But since the black-white problem is fairly widespread (most of the United States, Africa, Europe, Australia) let's generalize from it. The quest for rights for black people was the result of some white people exerting disproportionate amounts of power over black people. Since the civil-rights struggle has won passage of laws extending deserved rights to black people, there are whites who now claim an imbalance of power. They accuse the federal government of "bias" in favor of black people. Whites of low economic status, who found their only power in lording over blacks, feel particularly threatened, translating their fears into such prophecies as, "The blacks will take over" (which means, "usurp my power-position"). Hence, no progress in race relations can occur until white people abandon attempts to flaunt power over black people, and until black people reject the separatist mentality cloaking some areas of their community. Where there are separate kingdoms, there will be a continuing battle for one to establish dominance over another. On spaceship earth, and particularly in the narrow confines of a nation, neighbors simply don't have the luxury of perpetuating power exercises over one another.

Between Christians of different races, there should be the very clear recognition that God has called them as witnesses. That is, He has, by the inference of His specific call on individual lives, summoned us to show the world how our differences can be worked out (read: "powers can be balanced") through love and membership in one family— that of God. This means that each Christian participant should be working for power for his brother. There is no better route to an equalization of strength—economic, political, or otherwise!

But that requires abandonment of the sun-god, and a commitment to the God who demands the risk of being powerless. It is apparent that power struggles reach to every level of life. Man's only hope for liberation from the destructive demands of the power quest is by aligning his life with the One who shows how to be powerless in a world measuring its values by power, and the One who gives the paradoxical strength to be meek in such a world.

Zapping the spark out of the sun-god, ironically, is the God revealed in Jesus of Nazareth, known on occasion as the "meek and mild" One. The times in which Jesus talked about the poor being the most fulfilled and the meek inheriting the earth were not exactly characterized by gentleness. Roman eagles, then symbolizing earth's mightiest power, glared everywhere. The subjugated were themselves subjugating. Beggars and lepers were trash. Women were viewed with general scorn. Yet here came Jesus talking about meekness and poverty of spirit!

The meekness Jesus taught, lived, and empowered was characterized by nonarrogance in the face of arrogance. This was among the things that bugged the Pharisees and Sadducees about Jesus. They would come at Him with their little verbal webs, certain that He would be ensnared. Rather, in calmness, He would untangle their webs, answer their questions, and only further frustrate them.

One can visualize when they tried to trick Him into swearing allegiance for or against Caesar. Nonarrogantly, He asked for a coin. "Give to Caesar what is Caesar's, and to God what is God's" (see Luke 20:25).

There He was in the court of Pilate. A representative of the most arrogant power on earth, at that time, gazed on Him from a pedestal and He stood there and said nothing to defend Himself. What an incredibly risky business!

In the jargon of our time, Jesus Christ was one cool guy. In more traditional terms, maybe the best way to describe His manner is "holy confidence." Arrogance most often betrays fear or a passionate need to be admired because of a basic sense of inferiority. The Christian who has holy confidence has it because he knows he does not look to himself for ultimate assurance.

Not long ago, I went on an intellectual circus and spent an afternoon reading all about how flying saucers visited earth eons ago. Their inhabitants did such wondrous tricks that the poor earthlings proclaimed them gods, and lo and behold, there was the beginning of religion. I'm such a louse, I have a hard time going into such theories with an open mind. It's a risk to concede that. But I wasn't helped at all by the panicky arrogance of the theory's author. He has spent years dredging up bits and pieces of archeological data to support his ideas. But then he puts them forth in what is largely a diatribe against science and religion. The scientific world, he laments, will never give him the recognition he deserves. And religion—well, that's a fairy tale. The point is that if any man's foundations are weak, and he wants to peddle them anyway, his own fears are going to come through as arrogance. This is why a Christian utterly cancels the impact of his witness when he communicates it like a shaky witch docter trying to convince mankind he is the summation of all medicine!

As disciples of Jesus, let's be bold in spreading the message. But there's no need for us to be arrogant. In fact, it is counterproductive since it makes us look like we don't believe what we're saying. Remember, only the genuinely strong can risk thwarting the temptation to power.

The meek person, however, is not without spine. He is not a character who shuns totally the use of power. He recognizes that power is not always evil, and this gets to the core of the kind of meekness Jesus teaches and empowers. Being powerless, in the spirit of Jesus, is a qualitative, not a quantitative matter. It is an arrangement of priorities. It is knowing when to exercise power (or anger) and when not to. It is to make the proper selection of time and circumstances under which to use power. The time and circumstances, with the style of the exercise of power, determine whether or not it is immoral, according to the example of Jesus.

This is the point at which meekness becomes risky. The Christian is commanded not to use power indiscriminately, but to make a responsible choice. What are the guidelines for making such a choice? How is a Christian to know the circumstances under which the use of power is legitimate? The best way is to study the life of Jesus, and note the circumstances under which He did or did not use the vast power available to Him.

Two circumstances in which Jesus did not use His power teach us a lot. The first was in the wilderness, when He refused to cave in to the commands of Satan. The temptations have been interpreted in many ways. But it is clear there were three of them, and there is a sense in which they can be viewed as one. This one general temptation was for Jesus to manipulate power to satisfy His personal needs and wants.

The temptations doubtless had powerful impact on the human, hungry body of Jesus. It must have been tantalizing to know that by a simple piece of sideshow acrobatics, He could have the attention and following of the vast numbers of people to whom He preached. Satan appealed to Him in every instance to use the power at His disposal to meet the demands of His own nature. Jesus wanted to eat; He wanted to reach the people; He knew that He must be received as God's revelation if He was going to save them—but not on Satan's terms. What Satan ultimately hoped to get to was Jesus' ego. In essence, the devil was saying to Jesus: "You're not who you say you are until you prove it by doing those things I command you." Jesus established a principle for the usage of power when He refused to pervert power simply to satisfy ego and win recognition.

Who can say how much political scandal and stress on the democratic system could be avoided were that principle applied? How many wars could be avoided if men universally took to heart the principle. Homes and families might still be together if the factions could have seen they were violating this principle of power usage. Political parties, church denominations, nations might find new sources of unity if the people who make them up could understand that the power they are exerting against their fellows has as a primary goal the gratification of ego. But first it takes the risk of being powerless!

That other example of when Jesus did not use His power happened in Gethsemane. We focus on Jesus as He confronts death. Now is the pivotal moment. He can skirt it here, if He wants. Even if He waits until He gets on the cross to call a legion of angels, He still will have suffered the agony of being hung there. It is now or never if suffering is to be avoided. He disappears into the gentle vortex of the greenery to agonize over the horror that awaits Him. For a fleeting moment, Jesus thinks of the power available to Him. "If it be possible, let this cup pass from me. . . ." But then something else enters His mind. ". . . nevertheless not as I will . . ." (Matthew 26:39 KJV). What has happened in that flash to make Jesus yield? Quite simply this: He focuses outward, on the needs of others. There can be no salvation for mankind unless Jesus goes to the cross. Here He shows He will not use His power to save His own life when others are in need. But positively, He *will* give Himself for others, and the focus of His usage of power will be in the direction of the need of others.

What becomes clear is that Jesus will not use His power

for self-centered gains. Meekness is knowing when to use power. When the use is for the benefit of self at the expense of others, or of principle, then the power use is perverted.

There are two occasions when Jesus did use His power which have as much to say as those times when He did not. The first was the cleansing of the temple. To some, Jesus' act of driving out the money changers was a first-class contradiction. They wondered how He could teach the ideal of meekness, then apparently lose His temper.

But the temple incident was a clear sign that Jesus did not rule out anger or the use of power in anger. It did show, however, that the circumstances must be measured carefully. Jesus drove out the money changers because they were perverting the place of worship by shortchanging their customers. He sent them scampering because they were committing injustices against God and man. In the temple incident, Jesus was saying that He would use His power when the worship of God is perverted for men's selfish goals, and when injustices—deceptions—against men are rampant.

But, to repeat, we men must carefully measure our use of this kind of power. We must remember that Jesus Christ was probably the only person who ever lived who could boot somebody out of the temple in complete and total, objective love. He had a unique ability to make a clear judgment and condemnation of their sin. Our ability to judge is hedged by our own sin. The circumstances and motives under which we use power thus have a lot to do with it.

Dr. John Claypool has noted that secular power usage is usually determined by three types of values: those which are insensitive, self-serving, and materialistic. He observes also that the church, caught up in the mime of her culture, often works in the same way. There is nothing risky about being insensitive, self-serving, and materialistic. It isn't even a proper use of power in secular commerce, let alone in the church!

That's why Jesus, when He wanted to turn the earth inside out, chose people who had not a smidgin of power in earth's measurement. Indeed, the most powerful witness I ever knew was a frail disciple from Kashmir who laid the cement and brick for his church building with his own hands, then, because of his lack of power to get the government to change a tiny zoning law, had to rip it all down!

The most powerful churches in history have been those who really put their power on the line. These churches were assaulted and badgered. They wound up in the various lions' dens of their eras. But they became, as Elton Trueblood called them, "incendiary fellowships." They were powerless, yet their power was immeasurable. They had taken the risk of meekness. You and I, as disciples of Christ, are evidence that they inherited and are inheriting the earth.

5

THE RISK OF FOOLISHNESS

For me, that great edifice of mathematical wisdom assembled at such pain by wizards from Pythagoras to Einstein came tumbling down at age six, as if it had been a Tinker Toy tower. The credit for this intellectual devastation must go to Miss Moyer, a first-grade teacher who should have known better.

Arithmetic came about as easily for me as writing a dictionary for the proverbial monkey at the typewriter. I had struggled with the weird markings until broken with frustration. For such children, there should be a Rosetta Stone of arithmetic. Quite frankly, I had begun to assume Miss Moyer was an oracle, so I crept up to her desk to ask if I had worked my problems correctly. Then she did it. Before the whole class, she broke into a guffaw and proclaimed: "He doesn't even know what two plus two are." I squeaked, "Four," as I crawled back to my chair, scarlet with humiliation.

I have thought with some devilish appreciation that in the light of the new math, the Rosetta Stone of Miss Moyer had a glaring flaw. Two plus two do not invariably offer up four. And years later, in college new math, had I answered four to the riddle of two plus two, I would have flunked.

My wretched experience with arithmetic has done one good thing for me. It has brought me a deep awareness of and appreciation for 1 Corinthians 1:18: "For the preaching of the cross is to them that perish foolishness . . ." (KJV). And, as the New English Bible says it: "God has made the wisdom of this world look foolish" (verse 20).

Think of it: For ages, men have proclaimed that two plus two are four, that human knowledge has encompassed all that two plus two can ever be, that we expect to learn no more about two plus two, and that is that. On such a flimsy assumption, the pyramids were built (unless the Egyptians knew something we have only just learned), the Parthenon was raised, and Stonehenge mapped out. Then, poof! Out there in God's yet-to-be-fathomed universe, there is the truth that two plus two may not always be four, that it depends on the number system you're using. The Creator didn't do it that way for the vindication of a fat little schoolboy, but Hallelujah! anyway.

Actually, I'm a bit surprised that there has not already appeared a Two Plus Two Are Four Society with demands for reparations for arithmetic students everywhere who have flunked because they didn't know what two plus two was all about.

Anyway, the two-plus-two business underscores the irony of human beings trying to erect or perceive absolutes on their own. Some thinkers, for example, always seem to be bent on confounding the Scripture with the sweep of their knowledge, just about the time the Scripture is narrowing that sweep to the width of a thread.

"God has made the wisdom of this world look foolish": Have mercy on the Flat Earth Society, that strange assortment of Englishmen who still believe the earth is flat and that the visions of the astronauts are optical illusions.

"God has made the wisdom of this world look foolish":
Pity those trembling tyrants who dragged an apology out of
Galileo, but didn't hear him say he still believed his theory
anyway.

"God has made the wisdom of this world look foolish":
A final sorrowful nod to those who proclaim that God sim-
ply doesn't fit into their systems of epistemology, therefore,
He is not.

It is at this point, in fact, that the matter becomes tragic.
Were it not for the fact that, as Paul says, ". . . the world
failed to find [God] by its wisdom" (1 Corinthians 1:21 NEB),
man's whole pompous concept of his intelligence capabili-
ties would be comical. As it is, since he dismisses God as
blithely as he once did a round, sun-orbiting planet, the
thing turns to tragedy.

Goethe, in *Faust,* has Mephistopheles make a remark that
tells volumes about the cocky, but precariously narrow,
spirit of man: "I Though not omniscient, much to me is
known." But who needs Mephistopheles? The attitude is
lived out in millions of lives every day. "I may not know
everything, but what I do know makes up for what I don't
know."

Call it spiritual provincialism, but as I look back, this attitude was my infantile view of the world. I figured a seven-
hundred-mile slice of Dixie pretty much reflected everything else. It mattered little if I ever saw or learned anything
else about the earth. Then I saw the Alps. I flew up the
middle of Hong Kong harbor and watched mountains embrace sea. I squinted at a sunset over Bombay. More important, I walked back alleys in Seoul and New York and even
my own city, and stood nose to nose with despair. I saw

broken bodies in Asia and lonely, isolated elderly in Europe. And with each experience, at the eye of the emotional hurricane was the increasing awareness of my limitations, of my clumsy inadequacy to embrace the world and relieve its pain. My wisdom simply wouldn't measure to the task, and never will! Were it not for God, I would retreat to some chamber and pull the blinds on the world! I would become an Archie Bunker, and douse myself in all the narrowness and emptiness of my shallow skull. Or, I would become a dropout of the left, and scamper off to some commune in New Mexico. But God *is,* and despite the failure of my knowledge to probe Him out, He has made Himself known, and in doing so He has condemned my pettiness.

Ironically, though, when man fails to find God through his own wisdom, and hence shuts out God, he also shuts out the possibility of his own limitations. Look, for example, at Sigmund Freud. Man, he concluded, is a creature in search of a father, propelled by sex. God wouldn't fit in the package, but instead of digging around for a more adequate package, Freud threw out God—which is to say, "Look God, either you exist on my terms, or you don't exist at all."

This is as absurd as the fellow who decides he wants to give his kid a bicycle for Christmas. He wants to put the bicycle under the tree, all wrapped and tied in a yellow bow, in a nice box. The bicycle comes unassembled, and at the risk of sanity, the old man works late into the night rigging it. At last he gets the job done, and begins to stuff the bicycle back into the box, so it will be a surprise. But the handlebars and pedals, in their proper position on the bike, won't fit into the box. The man squirms and twists and even tries the hocus-pocus of some four-letter words, but the bicycle just won't go in the box. So, he throws away the bicycle and puts the empty box under the Christmas tree. Ridiculous? No more so than trying to dispense with God when He won't fit into our intellectual packaging.

Even religious men occasionally succumb to this weird twist. In the late sixties, for example, the theological problem was supposed to be in conceptualizing God. Dr. Altizer and friends decided that since they could find no point in their particular psyches at which they could come to a full conception of God, then the Deity must have died. The death-of-God kick ebbed into the linguistic crisis. Scholars stumbled around with the problem of words. Some concluded that it was really impossible to say anything "meaningful" (according to man's definition of "meaningful") about God, therefore talk about Him was a swim in futility. It was simply another way of throwing away the present because it wouldn't fit the package.

All of which leads to a better understanding of why Paul says, as the New English Bible words it, that God chose to save men by the "folly of the Gospel" (1 Corinthians 1:21 NEB). And what folly! The gospel is the story of a kid born on the backside of nowhere, whose youth is apparently so humdrum that nobody pays much attention to it, who grows up to be a calloused-hand carpenter (a thoroughly honorable occupation, but scarcely earthshaking), and who winds up executed as a common criminal. It's all so utterly foolish. Yet three days beyond the execution something even crazier happens, and two thousand years later this Carpenter is still around impacting and changing the lives of cynical men who have seen the other side of the moon!

The words of Abraham Lincoln and Teddy Roosevelt and Franklin Roosevelt and Woodrow Wilson and Harry S. Truman are as scratchy and forgotten as the old circumstances in which they were uttered. We've never seen Jesus, yet we seem able to perceive Him better than we can all those thousands of faces that have floated into our dens and living rooms every evening, but which are now as faded as old videotape. All those historical events which seemed so ultimate, so thorough in their implications for man and his future, have been exiled from our attention, even though once we thought we would never get over them. Gone is World War I's mustard gas, and flu epidemics and Teapot Dome and the Great Depression. Gone too are those things we thought we couldn't live without: Will Rogers and the Brooklyn Dodgers and nickle cigars. It's so foolish when you think about it. The ultimates of our generations tumble and dissolve in the acid of history, while the Carpenter of Galilee rides on and on, not only resisting history's efforts to put Him in His place (the human side of Him) but actually altering and supervising history!

It's no surprise, then, that the follower of Christ is going to risk looking pretty silly, by the world's standards. To be a Christian is to be immersed, not in what the world labels "cool reason," but in foolishness, and, at times, what the world might even consider insane scandal.

What is the nature of this "foolishness"? Well, for one thing, in a world like ours, it is to appear to be irrelevant. Hang on, now. I'm not saying the "foolish" gospel is irrelevant. I am saying that there are times when the Christian is going to look hopelessly irrelevant.

Heaven knows, most of us Christians perform exquisite little playlets to keep from looking irrelevant. Let somebody accuse the church of being irrelevant, and it is as if the Loch Ness monster rose from the lake and shouted, "Boo!" In the panic that follows, we seldom stop to ask if maybe it isn't the world out of sync rather than the church. Instead, we talk about letting the world set our priorities as if the world, like God, transcends time and space and has the last word on where it ought to go and how it ought to behave.

During my tenure, in the late sixties, as a religion editor, I covered the national conclaves of virtually every major denomination in America. The one game all were playing consistently was what I came to call the "relevancy match." A sort of unspoken challenge seemed to exist between the religious bodies, which said: "I can out-relevant you."

The easiest way to be relevant is to look relevant, decided some. Nuns threw away their habits. I ran into clergymen (WASPS, no less) who wore, above their clergy collars, Afro hairdos, and below the collar, red-striped bell-bottom trousers. Sculpture-cut got big with some denominations.

Then there were the experiments in worship. A number of denominations assembled in Milwaukee to experiment a bit. Among other things, the worshipers wound up snake-dancing in the church aisle. The World Library of Sacred Music published a manual of liturgical dance, called *Dancing for God*. The manual contained such swingers as "The Clergy Stomp" (not the kind practiced by some lay people).

There was also the "burning issues" syndrome, in which religious folk felt that they had to mutter something about everything because, like Mount Everest, the issues were there. This, even when the church folk had no more to say on some specific ambiguous topics than Huckleberry Finn to a brain surgeon.

It is not that the church is supposed to twaddle through culture, never saying anything. Quite the opposite! Christians ought to speak out, but not necessarily from the same perspective as *The New York Times* on one hand, and *The*

National Review, on the other. Tragically, often when the church speaks its collective voice on war, abortion, gay and women's liberation, it simply takes the theme already put out by secular commentators. The church has a perspective no other voice in society has; namely, the perspective of the Bible. And the world is in pitiful need of a fresh word on its problems.

Consider a bewildered physician I met once in Saint Louis. He was a delegate to the national get-together of his denomination. Just after a heated exchange on the convention floor over abortion, I spotted him wilting over lukewarm coffee in the pressroom. I walked up to get some first-hand quotes for the story I was about to file. "My church just told me I could do abortions, but they didn't tell me why," he said. And I knew what he was talking about. A host of secular commentators had come out favoring abortions, but this man felt the business of the church, rather than simply looking "relevant," was to comment on the ethics of the matter. In his mind, the church had copped out, and may as well have sent a letter to the editor of a newspaper which had come out for abortion, commending the stand.

I can't help but wonder: if, as Paul says, to be committed to Christ is to risk looking scandalous and foolish, doesn't this really mean that we might have to risk looking out of it (irrelevant) at times?

Kenneth Hamilton, of the University of Winnepeg, wrote an article sometime back for *Christianity Today* entitled, "The Irrelevance of Relevance." Dr. Hamilton's point was that relevance is really irrelevant if one wants to say anything in an absolute sense. There are, after all, some constants. Sometimes, the demand for relevance is for the readjustment of constant truth to new historical settings. Anything, according to this view, that does not relate to the present circumstance, is to be wiped out. What an incredibly pompous view! It is like saying ours is the only moment on the stage. It is even more narrow than that. It is like saying that all of reality exists for me in this particular microsecond.

That attitude, of course, is no more pompous than the book title Dr. Hamilton recalls seeing: *The God I Want.* "This seems to me to be the quintessence of the cult of relevance, revealing its idolatrous core. Faith starts, at the very least, from the wish to discover *The God I Must Acknowledge, Since He Is,*" says Dr. Hamilton.

The irrelevance of relevance is this: a man wants to measure a strand of rope, and he wants to come up with twelve feet. To do so, he doesn't stretch the ruler to suit the rope. The ruler contains the absolute truth about measurement. If it is adapted to what's to be measured, there is no absolute, and the ruler is without meaning. If, according to the ruler, the rope only measures ten feet, then the rope is irrelevant to the man's needs. But the ruler wasn't irrelevant; it simply expressed the truth.

Vernard Eller, the witty Brethren scholar, plainly calls it, "The Grand Irrelevancy of the Gospel." In his book *The Promise,* Eller sums up the present situation:

> Today more than ever it is apparent that we live in a frenzied world. Liberals are in a frenzy to eliminate war, poverty, and racism *now*—no matter how much ill will, backlash, militancy, and destruction are created in the process. Conservatives are just as frantic to 'save' law and order, public morality, the American way of life. And the demand that the church must become 'relevant' is nothing but a prod toward joining the stampede.

If a person is a mere "irrelevant" bump on the fabric of history, it is often said that he has "wasted his life." The risk of foolishness the disciple of Christ takes is also this: it is to risk being accused of wasting a life on nothing.

Interestingly enough, in its distorted values, the world has little problem with people who waste their lives on "something." The epitome of this "something"-wasted life—in my own experience anyway—was a crusty Malaysian sultan I visited one time. We had been admitted to his rotund presence only after coming to a firm agreement with tommy-gun-armed guards at his palace that we were not assassins. After a breakfast of scrambled eggs and sausage (in deference to his American guests), we listened patiently as the old man brought out the mental tintypes of a world that flourished fifty years ago. The closest we got to the present was when he took us to a balcony of his palace and told us how he had watched airplanes pound away at Singapore—which was just across a strait of water—during World War II. Even at that, we were still twenty-five years short of the present.

Then he bade us to his duck pond. There were great mallards from the north; exotic ducks from Asia squawked the mysteries of the Orient; a graceful pair who had once swum the Seine cut a tiny wake in the minilake. By now the sultan was in the world of the ducks. He bragged and cooed as if they were his grandchildren. The very core of his existence for the last quarter century had been the care and feeding of the feathery animals. Somewhere far off in the steamy innards of his capital city, a hungry baby wailed, and the response from the ruler was to send juicy tidbits skimming across the duck pond. Maybe he reasoned that the ducks would not grow up to steal his throne or kill his children. They only honked their hunger. Whatever the rationale, I couldn't help but think, in a place like this with needs that fester like a deadly wound, what an incredible waste of a life!

Nevertheless the sultan was widely admired. Even then he was earning a slot on the travel itineraries of the bored and beautiful jet setters who were always in search of something unusual to do, somewhere exotic to go. Even to them, it was probably clear that the sultan was wasting his life. But at least, maybe they reasoned, he was wasting it on "something."

The irony of it all was that there were missionaries in his country about whom some perhaps made jokes and dismissed as foolish people who had stuck themselves off in a corner of oblivion, sweating over people who were overpopulating the earth anyway. They were wasting their lives on "nothing," and that is unacceptable in a world for whom the part, something, is the whole, everything. Yet it was the missionary who, when the babies of the sultan's subjects wailed, showed their parents how best to satisfy the hunger. It was the missionary who would return in retirement to a land and people who had long since forgotten him. It was the missionary who, by his own choice, had made of himself an alien.

Paul Tillich called it "holy waste." His text was Mark's account of the woman who came with an alabaster jar filled with costly ointment, which she poured over Jesus' feet. The woman won Jesus' praise and the disciples' scorn. According to the standards the disciples were accustomed to measuring things by, dumping oil fit for an emperor on the dusty feet of a homeless carpenter was an absurd waste. And in their provincialism, the disciples were blinded to the larger truth: What the world considers sacrifice for value, and what God knows to be that sacrifice are often quite the opposite!

What waste, says the world, when a Telemachus jumps into the gladiatorial ring to condemn the slaughter in the name of God, and pays with his life. The world is staggered by the "waste" of a missionary like David Fite, who stays at his post in Cuba until Castro throws him in a prison. And there is Kagawa, "wasting" his life in the river slums of Tokyo, when he could have had fame and power.

Why in heaven's name did they behave like that? Because their lives were lived "in heaven's name," and because they were following the Christ of the cross, and the cross is "holy waste" in totality (see chapter seven). Tillich says it in *The New Being*: "The Cross does not disavow the sacred waste, the ecstatic surrender. It is the most complete and the most holy waste."

The life characterized by holy waste does not calculate the returns or cost of the love it pours out, and that is another reason the word "waste" is sometimes hung on the attitude of the Christ-follower. While working for the government, I occasionally became aware of the criteria used by federal agencies in making grants. The prime measure was a neat little stick, called the "cost-benefit ratio." That rule stipulated that the benefits derived from spending a certain amount of money would have to justify the expenditure.

Quite frankly, I was pleased to learn that the government, which was spending my money, took the long-and-measured view before it opened its purse. But cost-benefit ratios have no place in Christian discipleship and especially in the people aspect of God's church. That is, the Christ-follower never spends his love simply because someone might return it. The church shouldn't be in the business of primarily trying to recruit into its membership those who can contribute a lot in talent and money. The pattern, set by Jesus on the cross, is to spend agape love everywhere, irrespective of the return. It is to take the risk of looking like the mad millionaire, casting his precious dollars into the wind. The follower of Jesus is not called to measure mission against cost, or sowing against reaping. The disciple is, rather, one who blows the seed everywhere, believing that the seed of the Word never returns void. But it bears nothing until it is "wasted," and everyone knows that a wasteful person is a foolish person.

"Foolishness" was not the only word Paul picked to characterize the way the gospel, with its cross-message, looks to some. He also said it was *scandalon,* a "stumbling block" to the Greeks. And the "scandalous" nature of the gospel proclamation is just as much a stumbling block now, as well, and not only to Greeks. For whatever else that "scandalous" characteristic may be, it is the fact that the Christ-follower is audacious enough to claim that his Master is "the way, the truth, and the life," and, that "no man cometh unto the Father" but through the Christ (John 14:6 KJV).

An absolute truth!

One aspect of the somewhat mushy mysticism that has sprouted in the weed patch of post-World War II nihilism is the idea that all religions point with equal skill toward God, and that the prophets of all religions are somehow coequal. Jesus, Mohammed, and Buddha join with others in a kind of quasi-divine fraternity. Somehow, goes the theory, if all these religious figures could get together and focus their spiritual energies, the world would have an instant millenium, as tasty as the long-perked type. Into this spongy spirituality comes the follower of Jesus, reminding the world that Jesus was the one who claimed *He* was God become man, and the Christian doing that risks looking as scandalous as if he had worn combat boots to dinner at the Waldorf!

The audacity of the Christian message carries with it a particularly heavy risk of being scandalous now. The temptation to universalism, syncretism, is as beckoning as it was for the ancient Israelites. Now it is masked in virtues everyone wants: tolerance and intellectual honesty. Leonard Griffith cites the following examples in *Barriers to Christian Belief.* Norman Cousins has called for a World Parliament of Religions, and he urges that "the great religions cease explaining their differences to one another and begin to chart the elements of basic unity that would serve as building blocks of common action." When Paul Tillich, in 1950, was lecturing at Yale, he spent so much time talking about other faiths that the student newspaper headed an article: "Will Tillich come out for Christianity?" And the renowned historian Arnold Toynbee, in his *Study of History,* stated: "I reject the pretension of Christianity to be a unique revelation of the truth about Reality and a unique means of grace and salvation."

One wonders how such scholars can accept Christianity as one of the "great faiths" if its audacity, which is so clearly stressed, is so terribly off the mark. Either Jesus was the full revelation of God He claimed to be, or He was a demented liar.

If He was a demented liar, then He has no place in the pantheon of "great religious leaders."

The fact that the Christ-follower has a rather audacious claim to make for his Master doesn't give him a license to smugness, or cultural imperialism, or even intolerance.

Probably what turns off some people about the Christian claim is the tendency of some Western Christians to believe that God's command to spread the gospel means also the mandate to export Western culture. This is imperialistic indeed, and has no place in a faith, which, if it had any cultural foundations at all, would be those of the Middle East.

The world is terribly reluctant to commit itself in an absolute way, or to something it considers "narrow." But there are some absolutes, and the foundational one is that *the* way rebellious, spiritually confused people get united with God is through the binding agent He stipulated: Jesus Christ, the God-man who died on a cross for mankind. All other religious leaders have died, but none of them have claimed that their deaths were the agent of humanity's redemption. And even at that, the real audacity of the Christian message doesn't rest in the claim, but in the emptiness of Christ's tomb! There are few scandals to exceed that.

Much of the dilemma facing the individual Christian and the church at present is a result of the sweeping complexification in modern life. Everything seems awash in ambiguity. Upward-bounding populations, intricate issues have rendered some forms of government obsolete. Scientific discovery and technical innovation increase man's options for improving the quality of his life, but stupefy him with the demands for proper choices of gadgets and even goals. Development of psychological and social sciences have left people wondering not only who their neighbors are, but who *they* are, personally. Into this web of confusion and complexity comes the Christian, proclaiming the basic simplicity of the gospel. And this is part of the risk of foolishness: to proclaim simplicity in a world which is not only complexifying, but is proud of its complexity, confusing complexity with progress.

It is helped along the way by some theologians, like the great Jesuit Teilhard de Chardin. Teilhard was a brilliant man, and it is a genuine shame the world can't relax on the soap-job he did on the problem of complexification. Taken as biology, perhaps, Teilhard's view is not so disturbing. Applied to social relationships, and that ultimate relationship between God and man, it is inadequate.

Teilhard envisioned creation as an ever-complexifying process, in which life folded upon itself again and again. Biological complexification brought human consciousness and human consciousness brought spiritual complexification, in Teilhard's scheme. Complexifying life moves in stages, he thought. The ultimate destination is a wonderful peak called "Christogenesis." At this stage, all creation is caught up in the Christ, in an evolutionary sense. As Teilhard saw complexification, every life action contributes and relates to the whole. It is as if he had applied Hobbes's theory of bumping atoms to the whole of life. Complexification, à la Teilhard, was a process to be greeted with enthusiasm.

The only hang-up with the whole scenario seems to be history and human experience. Man may be coasting merrily to Christogenesis via the broad highway of complexification, but he certainly seems to behave strangely for a Christogenesis-bound traveler. There are those, of course, who look back across history and conclude that modern man at this end of the evolutionary-complexification process is indeed much better than his simpleton ancestors. We do build hospitals and schools and give women and minorities the ballot. But can we really say we're all that much better? It seems, rather, that man is as barbaric as ever, he's just found cleaner ways of killing. An atom bomb is not nearly so dirty as a knight's ax, but it is considerably more deadly. Napalm spilled out of a B–52 is really no different from boiling pitch spilled off a castle battlement, except in the technical complexity of the delivery system and chemical structure. By these criteria, complexity has added little to virtue. It takes all the hospitals and orphanages in all the world to begin to balance the sheet against only one atomic bomb!

Perhaps no modern event shows the emptiness of the promise of complexification more clearly than the case of Lt. William Calley and the abomination of My Lai. The leading pundits spewed volumes of surprised and shocked and indignant rhetoric when the graves were opened. They were shocked because they had apparently concluded that man had arrived at such a wonderfully complex elevation that he could exist daily midst unleashed savagery without himself becoming a savage. While it is true that the only thing standing between civilization and the jungle is the complexity of the lawn-mower engine, the evidence is lacking that complexity has done all the good for man that Teilhard thought it would.

One of the most interesting episodes of the now defunct (but occasionally rerun) television show "The Outer Limits," dealt with the touted wonders of complexification. A simple Welsh coal miner fell into the hands of a scientist who used him as a guinea pig for experiments. The scientific dillydallying began a process in the coal miner in which he skimmed across the evolutionary fabric. A few hours after the initial experiment, his brain had complexified and grown larger, and he was consuming volumes of books in milliseconds. Still later, he complexified more, and became a cold mechanism who killed through thought. He began hunting some poor, simple humans of current vintage. Just as he caught up with one of his victims, he skipped across another evolutionary span, and to the joyful relief of the hunted man, evolved into a state of absolute mercy.

Walter Lippman probably had better insight into the truth of complexification when he wrote about the unease in American life he saw in the sixties. In the New York *Herald Tribune* Lippman wrote:

> The malady is caused, I believe, by the impact of science upon religious certainty and of technological progress upon the settled order of family, class and community. The "virtual despair" comes from being uprooted, homeless, naked, alone and unled. It comes from being lost in a universe where the meaning of life and of the social order are no longer given from on high and transmitted from ancestors but have to be invented and discovered and experimented with, each lonely individual for himself.

Presently, complexification is a cause and effect of quantification. As the totality of man's environment quantifies, it becomes more complex. In response, man complexifies his ways of relating to the greater quanities. The tragedy is that such complexification tends to become a blanket hiding more elemental truths. Take, for example, higher education. Following the scare thrown into our educational systems by the bleeping Sputnik in 1957, there was a panic to quantify education, particularly in technological areas. New questions began to be raised about education in general, as a result of the revolution of quantification; questions such as: Is it really the responsibility of the educational system to help develop moral values, or simply to transfer a quantity of data? Unfortunately, too many specialists decided that education and value-building was a poor marriage.

The quantification of education, since it was characterized by the rejection of any ethical or "spiritual" responsibility, was right in the tone of secularization, which, by the
late sixties, Harvey Cox had pronounced as holy anyway.
But unfortunately, the ultimate truth of quality, so simple
and so basic, was covered up. The truth of quality held, as
it always had, that quantification of the strictly material is
always dangerous without a parallel progress in qualification. Applied to the science of our time, qualification says
this: While you're teaching people the skills of constructing
wondrous new machines, you'd better be teaching them
some values that will enable them to make moral use of their
new machines. In other words, teach the button-pushers the
best circumstances and reasons under which to push the
buttons!

In retrospect, the student uproar of the late sixties, while
having specific causes like the Vietnam war, probably had
its foundations in the quantification in the universities. While
the methods and style of the unrest were deplorable, the
questions the students raised were worth society's paying
some attention to. At the heart of what many of them were
saying was the complaint that the universities, with all their
complexities, were doing little to give a sense of meaning
and purpose. What point, after all, is there in learning
greater quantities of data about life if life has no meaning,
no purpose, no lasting goals?

What does all of this have to do with the risk of foolishness taken by the Christian? Just this: Complexification, even
when it is demonic and disruptive, has the smack of sophistication, and is an irresistable urge in organized society, to
the extent that the person committed to something which,
at its base, is simple, is going to look quite foolish.

A world that drools its pride in the complexity of its

knowledge and structures is going to want to gain heaven through a complex religion. When the Christian comes proclaiming the basic simplicity of Christ's message—that salvation comes through trust in Jesus—the world is going to want to bolt for the guru's mountain and chant mantras and dip in holy rivers and think intelligible thoughts. If everything else is complex, and complexity seems so inherently good, why shouldn't our religion be complex? it will ask.

But the simple means of uniting God and man remains: Jesus died, was resurrected, and beckons to man. And the continuing thrust is simple in statement: "Seek ye first the kingdom of God, and His righteousness . . ." (Matthew 6:33 KJV). The other (complex) things will then fall into proper place. Or, as William Barclay translates Matthew 6:33:

> Make the Kingdom of God,
> and life in loyalty to him,
> the object of all your endeavour,
> and you will get all these other things as well.

God's promise?

Christlike simplicity is living fettered by nothing but God's purpose. Bonhoeffer said, in *Ethics,* it is "to fix one's eye solely on the simple truth of God at a time when all concepts are being confused, distorted and turned upside-down." The follower of Jesus is not called to turn his life over to a complex set of principles, but to a person—the Christ. True, creeds and principles may grow from that initial and basic personal commitment. But even then, the Christ-follower risking simplicity is able to break such creeds if they block or try to usurp Christ.

The person who goes around behaving irrelevantly by the world's standards, who is scandalous in his audacity, who "wastes" himself on "immeasurable nothings," who sees ultimates in simple terms when the "serious" world knows anything worthwhile is complex, is going to look like, well, a foolish clown. On the back of Harvey Cox's book *The Feast of Fools* is a picture of Cox and his family, donned in clown suits. But to risk being the fool for Christ, it is not really necessary to wear a clown suit. All that is required is to be committed to Christ. To the world, that's foolishness enough.

6

THE RISK OF CONFLICT

The Promised Land never was Placid Acres, but you'd never know it to hear some folks talk. To them, the Christian experience is a walk through Forest Lawn, the taking up of residence beside Lake Bliss, complete with Walt Disney singing trees and dancing birds.

What a shock, then, when such folk awake to the fact that being related to Christ is no opiatelike experience at all, but the kind of life which often seems to be at the abyss of risking conflict!

This is one reason I have such a massive hang-up about the Cecil B. DeMille/Charlton Heston version of a prophet. The DeMille/Heston prophet is always captured in profile —a stong, leading chin, arching chest, and eyes as stable as granite. The Hollywood-manufactured prophet always strikes me as a man with his feet implanted solidly in terra firma, sure of his future steps.

But how unlike the real nature of a prophet. A prophet is a man who has trouble sleeping at night. His spirit is an Armageddon of conflict. He tears himself over the love of his people and the love of his God. His eyes are minifurnaces, glowing so intensely that at times people mistake the prophet for being insane. His voice rasps. He is known to weep. The real prophet sees visions, labeled by some as the delusions of a demented man, as with Isaiah's view of God "high and lifted up," surrounded by seraphim. At other times, a prophet is a man like Hosea, crawling in shame into the marketplace to buy back his prostitute wife off the auctioning block. Sometimes the prophet sits like a fool under a tree—like Jonah—waiting for a signal from heaven.

More than all else, the prophet is a man of conflict. Sometimes his spirit becomes so brittle with the tension of this conflict, it would snap were it not for the stabilizing presence of God. The prophet, as Helmut Thielicke puts it in *The Trouble With the Church,* "had to learn in his own person to cope with the apocalyptic situation which threw the average person into shock, panic, or numbness and see it *sub specie aeternitatis*—simply because he had to climb up a pulpit or some makeshift platform to tell his beaten and beleaguered listeners that all this bad had something to do with God, with his judgement and visitation."

There are those people who, shortly after entering the Kingdom, get the distinct impression they went through the wrong door. These types were usually convinced that their prime calling as a Christian was to sit under a waterfall—well, to do the Western equivalent anyway—and wait for their souls to be washed over in that dreamy kind of conjured peace moviemakers convey by putting rose-colored filters on their camera lenses. But as their commitment deepens, they find a strange thing happening: there is a sense of peace over the security of the soul; and the better they get to know Jesus, they find the points of potential conflict in their lives multiplying. Thank God for the prophets. They let us know in such circumstances that everything is developing on track.

Marx said that religion is the opiate of the people. He was certainly an errant generalizer. But there are those who see religion primarily as the means to a good trip. Having this objective for one's faith corrupts the meaning of true religion. But take a Timothy Leary, for example. Leary was the apostle of the religious experience via LSD. What Leary was preaching by implication was that the sole purpose of religion is ecstasy. And if you couldn't get the "faith" on your own, baby, Father Timothy could point the way to the kingdom through his magic chemicals. Authentic faith supplies its share of bliss, but it punctuates a believer's life with conflict. The religious type trying to avoid a religion of conflict may as well rest his soul in the cuddly bosom of the Boston Uplift Society.

This is one of the things that makes so tragic the flight of many modern young people to the Eastern mystery religions. It's very doubtful that when Mia Farrow, the Beatles, et al., went to India in search of the guru, they were searching for conflict.

The world knows basically two kinds of religion. One, the nirvana religions, belongs essentially to the East. "Nirvana" is derived from the Buddhist term for salvation. Nirvana comes after lengthy contemplation. It brings a release from physical awareness, and a sort of holy numbness. The nirvana manifestation is seen in other forms of Eastern religions and quasi-religious practices—like Yoga. In the nirvana religions, one identifies with God through contemplation. Regardless of whatever happens as an end result, the experience is a highly self-centered one since most often the seeker of salvation has to exclude the rest of humanity from his eyes in order to save himself.

The religions of the West, namely Christianity and the

assorted spin-offs, are basically religions of the "Law," to use John Steadman's term (in *The Myth of Asia*). While the seeker of God going the nirvana route tries to find Him through contemplation, "the religion of Law seeks to accomplish the divine will through obedient action," according to Steadman. At the risk of sounding spiritually chauvinistic, one can understand why a generation of folk raised to think of instant and painless salvation—thanks largely to the influence of their tutelage by television—might find the Eastern religions attractive. There is the romantic lure of the bearded guru, meditating in a balmy jungle. There is the exotic feel of being able to say, upon return, "I was there. . . ." There is the sense of escaping the dull, slow process of obedience. Most of all, there is the relief of evading the conflict implanted in a person by the One who said, "I come not to send peace, but a sword" (Matthew 10:34 KJV). Any guru having made such a statement would be driven to hock his cow to survive!

The point is, Jesus said just that: "I come not to send peace, but a sword." And how that did prove true in the lives of His followers!

The classic example of this conflict on the personal level is Paul. The Saul in him just kept wanting to come out. Paul was to learn that Damascus Road experiences sometimes constitute the beginning of a long and agonizing warfare on the personal level. In his letter to the Romans, Paul skims along with an essay on the law, when the consciousness of the battle raging within himself stabs him to inject abruptly:

> We know that the law is spiritual; but I am not: I am unspiritual, the purchased slave of sin. I do not even acknowledge my own actions as mine, for what I do is not

what I want to do, but what I detest. . . . The good which I want to do, I fail to do; but what I do is the wrong which is against my will; and if what I do is against my will, clearly it is no longer I who am the agent, but sin that has its lodging in me.

I discover this principle, then: that when I want to do the right, only the wrong is within my reach. In my inmost self I delight in the law of God, but I perceive that there is in my bodily members a different law, fighting against the law that my reason approves and making me a prisoner under the law that is in my members, the law of sin. Miserable creature that I am, who is there to rescue me out of this body doomed to death?

                                    Romans 7:14–24 NEB

[handwritten margin note: How very human Paul was! How real! How easy to identify with!]

Paul answers his own question paradoxically: Christ can deliver him from the dilemma; yet, it is really Christ who brings the dilemma. If Paul had never met Jesus, the Saul within him would have been content to go his way. There would have been no conflict.

So what Paul made was a fatalistic concession of sorts. He knew that Christ would bring his soul the peace of security. But Paul surrendered himself to the war that would rage between the competing elements within himself. As Reginald White says it in *Apostle Extraordinary*:

> Well, let me sin, but not with my consenting,
>   Well, let me die, but willing to be whole:
> Never, O Christ,—so stay me from relenting,—
>   Shall there be truce betwixt my flesh and soul.

To be sure, the pagan Greeks felt an inner warfare. Plato wrote of the raging horses that attempted to pull the chariot of man's life up and down all at once, guided safely only by a wise and rational charioteer—the human will. And there is the spectacle of Orpheus, tooting desperately on his lute to keep his sailors from hearing the seductive wails of the Sirens.

But for the pagan Greeks, the conflict stemmed from their idea of the duality of life: that matter was essentially evil, and that spirit was good. Life must be a struggle to get away from the conflict produced by the duality of matter and spirit. Here is where the Christian like Paul differed radically from his pagan Greek contemporaries. Paul agonized over the conflict of good and evil battling within himself, and then opened himself to the possibility of more conflict by plunging deeper into his relationship with Christ! Orpheus kept piping; Paul threw his life to Christ and the multiplication of the points of conflict.

The nature of this conflict on a personal level stems from the very way in which a person enters a relationship with Christ. Gross misunderstanding about the style of entry into the Kingdom has resulted in the assumption that one can relate to Jesus in the nominal way he may relate to Amy Vanderbilt's good manners. Jesus described the nature of the beginnings in Him, and it is recorded in Luke 16:16: "Until John, it was the Law and the prophets: since then, there is the good news of the kingdom of God, and everyone forces his way in" (NEB). Or, as William Barclay translates the last phrase, ". . . everyone tries to storm his way into it."

Perhaps Elton Trueblood captures the thrust of Jesus' statement in *The Yoke of Christ* when he renders the phrase: ". . . everyone enters it violently." Trueblood says it's like a jet airplane breaking the sound barrier, creating a sonic boom. The idea could also be expressed by the reentry of a space vehicle into earth's atmosphere. It plunges from the tranquility of outer space into a burning confrontation with the elements comprising the atmosphere. Were it not for the protective heat shield on the space capsule, the astronauts would be parched.

The entry into the Kingdom as described by Jesus can be seen in yet another way. Sometime back, I was crossing the border of West Germany into Austria. The transition was a fairly simple one. I produced my passport, changed some currency, and was on my way. But the entry into the Kingdom is more like an illicit crossing from East Berlin to West Berlin. It is the picture of the young man I remember leaping from a fifth-floor window over the Wall, and screaming, *"Freiheit"*—"freedom." Whatever the symbolism used, the idea Jesus is conveying is the tearing movement from one life-style to another radically different one.

"Crisis" is not too strong a word to characterize the process of entering a relationship with Christ. It is the deep crisis produced when one stares nose to nose with the truth of Jesus. It is a crisis because that truth reveals the fact that the life-style one settled into like a comfortable pair of slippers before he met Christ, is totally inadequate. How disconcerting to discover that the way a person chose to carry himself through history was the wrong one!

One knows the inadequacy of a life-style only because there is the truth of a better alternative. There is a divisive nature for this truth. One confronts it, and must accept it or reject it. He must feel within himself the pang of warfare, of conflict. The Pharisees and Sadducees heard the truth and were disturbed by it. Why else would they plot the death of the messenger? The Samaritan woman heard the truth too, and her disturbance was so great, she dropped her water jugs and ran off to the village to announce the One had come who could not only give the right answers, but raise the deepest questions (*see* John 4).

Nicodemus heard, too, and he was told that entering into the new life is a birth process. It is not stillbirth. It is that coming into life punctuated by screams and anguish. C. S. Lewis, author of *Surprised by Joy,* got a hint of the conflict that lies in the path of entry into the Kingdom, but found himself "a prodigal who is brought in kicking, struggling, resentful, and darting his eyes in every direction for a chance of escape."

That is only the beginning. The developing nature of the Christian life, or growth, is in actuality a deepening of the commitment to Christ. That deepening is a process something like the explosion of an incendiary bomb. The birth into the Kingdom is the concussion, but the concussion is not the conclusion: next come the tremors and the flames.

Jesus said, "I have come to set fire to the earth, and how I wish it were already kindled! . . . Do you suppose I came to establish peace on earth? No indeed, I have come to bring division" (Luke 12:49, 51 NEB). And it is on that intimately personal level of a man's spirit that the fire rages most intensely.

How Simon Peter did burn! An impetuous talker, Simon, after his conversion, could have understandably greeted each day with a battle cry. So shaky was the man, the disciples might have been caught chuckling when Jesus told Simon, after his confession of the lordship of Christ, that from then on his name would be "Rocky" (*see* Matthew 16:16–19). Not the least of the postconversion wars Peter had to fight in himself was one over racism. The conflict

raged through noon one day at Joppa when God hurled
Peter into a trance and laid a clear order on him: Don't call
anyone or any creature "unclean" that God has created
(see Acts 11). And that took in the whole spectrum of
creation. But what burning inner conflict it took for Peter to
get the message!

One of the persisting metaphors for the process of Christian growth is that of death to life, or destruction to con-
struction. Being related to Christ is being immersed in the
conflict of permitting the old structures of what is at the
essence of a man's being to be stripped away so that they
can be replaced with new ones. The conflict is stirred over
watching cherished ideas and relationships swept into oblivion and feeling the birth pangs of new and mysterious ones
taking their place.

The conflict forged in the spirit of a Christ-follower stems
as much as anything from the awesome goals pursued. Jesus
challenged His followers to keep moving toward perfection
—even as God is perfect. And for Paul, chasing those goals
was best described in conflict terms—a competitive race. "I
press toward the mark" (Philippians 3:14 KJV). And one can
see the ancient racer, his body stripped and oiled, hearing
the breathing of his competitors at each side, but keeping his
eyes fixed on the ribbon stretched across the finish line
ahead.

A youngster named Timothy chased after Paul in the race,
and the battle-scarred apostle let him know he was not out
on a Sunday-afternoon hike. "Take your share of hardship,
like a good soldier of Christ Jesus," Paul wrote him (2 Timothy 2:3 NEB). And a good measure of that hardship is going
to be on the personal level, Paul said. Among other things,
Timothy, the fledgling servant of Christ, would have to hack

out some clear notion of his identity in the new Christ perspective. "A soldier on active service will not let himself be involved in civilian affairs; he must be wholly at his commanding officer's disposal" (verse 4). In other words, Timothy, battle out the question: Am I a soldier of Christ or not? And if you're a soldier of Christ, you've got to defeat all those penchants to go marching after different drummers. This idea would also have some import for Timothy's (and Christians' in general) relationship with his culture, as we'll see later. But coming to a decision about who's going to call the shots in the war called life is, of itself, a Battle of Gettysburg proportions.

But the conflict is a productive one. Just how this dynamic conflict works when it is fired by the Holy Spirit (conflict is a negative when the Holy Spirit is not in charge) I can't tell. My experience with psychology is limited to one college minor, which makes me as qualified to do psychoanalysis as listening to a record makes one able to teach music.

Besides, when the Holy Spirit works, analysis is an art not easily practiced, simply because we finite humans are hard put to explain just how God does anything. But the work of the Holy Spirit is reportable. That's what preaching and witnessing are all about. So, in relating just how the conflict induced by Jesus in the life of a disciple is productive, let me be reporter rather than psychologist.

The fellow's name is disguised. We'll call him Sam. When I met Sam, we were serving together on the White House staff. He was young and aggressive. Sam crouched at the threshhold of his career like a racer in starting position. At the White House in those days, we occasionally had informal prayer breakfasts for members of the staff. Sometimes Sam came. He was always fishing around on the periphery of the Gospel.

During this period, though, Sam was embroiled in conflict. Like so many of those who serve at high levels of government, Sam was being consumed by his job. His family was coming apart. Sam's buoyant stride was giving way to the sag of a spent warrior, a vanquished veteran. The conflict continued until finally Christ broke through Sam's life, through the witness of some committed businessmen in Washington. Sam didn't stop the war inside himself. Rather, he changed directions, and found himself girded with a new battle suit. One day Sam and I sat in a conference in a Washington hotel, and I heard him tell the men that man's extremity is God's opportunity.

I thought, ah yes. When man has flayed and stabbed with his meager sword, and the conflict has backed him up against an impregnable wall, God can swoop into his life. He doesn't end the war, but reequips the warrior and sends him charging off after the enemy—this time on the offensive.

Once a person has plunged into the Christ-commitment and taken the risk of personal conflict, he often finds that the new focus of conflict, while it continues within himself, is with his culture.

Being in conflict with one's culture doesn't automatically make one a Christ-follower. One would hardly characterize Vladimir Lenin or Genghis Khan as being disciples of Jesus. But they were as out of sorts with general culture as men have ever been. Conflict—the bloody kind—dogged their ugly tramps through history. Again, the essential difference between the Christian in his conflict with culture and the likes of the men named above, is the Holy Spirit. God works conflict into something constructive. Subtract His guidance and the result is destructive.

The most basic level at which the Jesus-follower finds this

cultural conflict is with particular people and groups. Malcolm Muggeridge, on "rediscovering Jesus," found that
some of his old associates treated him as if he had been
arrested "for indecent exposure in Hyde Park." The former
editor of *Punch* and rector of Edinburgh University was
labeled "mad." Further, says Muggeridge in *Jesus Rediscov-
ered:*

> The commonest opinion is that with advancing years I
> have gone soft and become a bore—two perfectly plausi-
> ble judgments; a more implausible one is that I have suc-
> cumbed to the lures of the Establishment. Would it were
> so, and I had been endlessly rejecting offers of life peer-
> ages, OBEs, honorary degrees and invitations to dine with
> the Fellows of All Souls! Alas, far from it. I have to disclose
> that since I began to try to be a Christian and endlessly talk
> about it, the chilliness with which I have long been re-
> garded in Establishment circles has turned into a positive
> ice age."

It was as much for Joe Q. Christian as for Brother Malcolm
that Paul enjoined, "Come out from among them, and be
ye separate . . ." (2 Corinthians 6:17 KJV). This conflict with
particular people is not only the most basic, but often the
most difficult. One can imagine the tremors that must have
hounded through Saint Augustine that day, after his conversion, when he bumped into one of his former mistresses.
Tradition says the bishop of Hippo had mistresses when he
was fifteen years old. He would have been known in our
day as a real swinger. Then God thrust Augustine into battle.
On the day of that chance encounter, the heart of the
ex-mistress thudded with anticipation as she said, "Augus-

tine, it is I." And God's Augustine replied, "Yes, but it is not I."

There have been those proof-texters who have wanted to make that admonishment to "be separate" mean something racial, or economic, or cultural. But the thrust of the order is that the Jesus-follower has to separate himself from the ideals and goals and practices of those whose allegiance belongs to someone or something other than Jesus. If it were physical separation, Jesus would not have talked so much about risking being present in the world as we discussed a few chapters back. Nor would there be any room for conflict if we Christians were all up on Nirvana Peak and the nonbelievers remained in the valley.

No, our command is to be present with people who don't follow Christ, but to separate ourselves from what they are and what they stand for. Sometimes, of course, we find they separate themselves from us while we battle to cling to a relationship with Christ and identify with the world, simultaneously.

I spent seven years trying to plod through life like that. With one hand, I thought I was representing Christ. With the other, I dallied with the old relationships. The rationale was neat, all tied up in colorful ribbons: I would identify with the "world" so that my witness would be credible. At long last, it occurred to me that my very identification was what was making my witness noncredible. Those "worldly" folk, while labeling me as one of the gang, expected someone who occasionally muttered prayers to be different. If I wasn't "separate" (different) why should they turn to the Christ I mentioned, since it apparently had made only a modicum of difference in my own life? Doggone good question.

Conflict with particular people and groups for the follower of Jesus is perfectly natural. It should be. Jesus experienced it from the outset of His ministry, and with His own family, no less. One day Jesus was preaching in Galilee, when He was interrupted in midspeech. "Your mother and brothers are outside, and want to speak to you," said the messenger. Jesus looked around and responded: "Who is my mother? Who are my brothers? . . . Whoever does the will of my heavenly Father is my brother, my sister, my mother" (Matthew 12:49, 50 NEB).

It must have been like my friend, George. One dazzling summer afternoon he cut off his thumb with a lawn mower. The weeks of recuperation dragged like a turtle band. After a while the pain and frustration drove him out of his mind, and I awoke one morning to George's rasping voice screaming to God, his neighbors, and anyone passing within five blocks of the front yard, which was the stage of his madness. Quietly the family led him into the house. Later in the day, the cars began arriving as the relatives went into counsel about what to do. George went through shock treatments, and a few months later was as sane as anyone else on the block.

So Jesus' family can be imagined, assembling outside the building where their son and brother was playing out His "madness." They couldn't even bring themselves to enter and lead Him away. Jesus became the first to live through the conflict He had already talked about:

> I have come to set a man against his father, a daughter against her mother, a young wife against her mother-in-law; and a man will find his enemies under his own roof.
>
> Matthew 10:35, 36 NEB

It dosen't have to be so. <u>All it takes is a united commitment to Christ for a family to discover peace beyond its most fancied dreams. But always there is the risk of conflict.</u>

How 2 pray for this !!!

The risk of conflict with particular people is always haunting the Christian because, quite simply, the Christ-follower has a different set of standards than his culture in general. When there is an absence of conflict between Christ's people and their culture, it may be time for some questions, such as, are we as Christians really in conflict with culture's assumption that material success is the world's greatest good?

The verbiage of Christendom overflows with tithing testimonies beginning, "I tithe because God always pays me back, in a bigger way. . . ." Churches take out half-page ads announcing that last Sunday they had three thousand people in Sunday school. Wonderful. Except at times such achievement is not so much because God is pouring out His blessing as it is that some churches just know more about gimmickry, like donkey rides, Green Stamps, and assorted other tricks which would shame your friendly neighborhood flimflam man. And there is the eternal maxim that if a church has been able to raise the biggest building around, God must be present all over the place.

He may very well be, just as the three thousand in Sunday school may have been gathered by His Spirit. But the church is not Chase Manhattan and <u>material success must never be the standard by which it decides if it is effectively doing God's work</u>. After all, there are times when crucifixion, a tearing away, a rending asunder, may be the mark of God's pleasure. That's hard to buy unless a collection of God's people known as the church understand they are in conflict with secular culture's assumptions about material things.

But there is another question for the disciple of Jesus: Are we as Christians really in conflict with culture's penchant to assign to itself messianic scope?

In secular culture, both right and left often behave as if the ultimate answers rested on their deeds and sayings. Too often, churchmen are prone to go chasing after cultural fads with the zest of a spinster in pursuit of a comfortable companion.

On the right, for example, there are collections of Christians for whom the nation's flag is only a little lower than the cross. The founding fathers are near-deities. The country's leadership is regarded in almost holy intonations.

Nor is the left immune. Churchmen of that stripe have often outlined the Brothers Berrigan, the Daniel Ellsbergs, and other figures with an aura resembling holiness. Many of them nodded sad assent when George McGovern talked of his defeat as being the nation's loss, as if we had had the chance to put holiness in the White House and blown it. And some church people in the United States stumble over one another seeking proximity to the throne of Angela Davis.

Now again, as with material success as a measure, such phenomena may have their degree of correctness, but the follower of Jesus must never find himself in such frozen allegiance to the ideas and leading figures of his culture that he lapses into giving them messianic standing. The Christ-follower is ever at conflict with such notions.

A question remains for the Jesus-disciple in conflict with the values and ideals of his culture: Are we as Christians sacrificing our integrity before Christ on the altar of cultural tradition?

The mandate to the Christian and the church in which he

gathers with others of like mind is not to be a rubber stamp of the traditions of his society, unless, of course, those traditions are patterned on Jesus' teachings. But tragically, how often the witness of communities of Christians has been diluted because they were too quick, as units, to endorse cultural practices anathema to Jesus' teachings!

Once, as a newspaperman, I was writing a long piece about how far a certain city had come in race relations. I was questioning a community leader about the lag in his organization's progress in giving policy-making roles to minorities. The fellow knew me, and knew that I was a minister. "Mr. Henley," he thundered, "a bunch of your churches won't even admit certain minorities as members and *you're* questioning the progress of *my* organization?"

An evasion, to be sure. But, sadly, his point was well taken. I heard him: You guys in the church are supposed to be the moral pacesetters. How can you expect the community to be any better than its churches? And there were secondary questions, like: Doesn't this mean, then, that the church should be challenging, within the framework of the Gospel of Christ, cultural tradition, rather than sometimes using that Gospel to support it? How the risk of conflict does shoot upward!

Despite the notion that the only thing certain in life is death and taxes, there is another sure thing for the Christperson: The Christian in conflict with his culture will, at some point, find himself in conflict with, or because of, his state.

Maybe the initial conflict is over whether or not or to what degree a Christian should involve himself with politics and affairs of government. Theodore Roosevelt once remarked that a man who calls politics a cesspool and then

refuses to get involved because it is a cesspool, is a hypo-
crite. Perhaps that is reason enough for the Christian to get
involved. But there are better ones.

When Jesus gave His followers their marching orders
prior to His ascension, in the Great Commission, He commanded that as they went, they should evangelize. He
meant, therefore, that in the professions we find ourselves,
our major objective is to present the gospel to people. Elton
Trueblood says that the ways we earn our living are our
"other vocations," our central one being that of witness.

Perhaps it is tragic that the Christian should even have to
ask himself the question of involvement, because, in its
purest form, politics should be the art of servanthood. Politics has been defined as a means of combining testy and
competitive human wills into actions that will benefit all.
Perhaps the question politics is supposed to help answer is
this: How can conflicting human ambitions be woven together with a minimum of disorder and violence?

Viewed that way, can a Christian really avoid politics and
be loyal to his commitment of being the conduit through
which Christ injects His characteristics of love, justice, and
mercy into the world?

The ancient Christian Tertullian saw it otherwise. He
wrote: "We (Christians) have no inducement to take part in
your public meetings; nor is there aught more entirely foreign to us than affairs of state." Tertullian's view, in essence,
seemed to regard culture almost through Gnostic eyes, as if
culture were the creation of some demonic force. And to
the extent that men are possessed by the demonic, it was
and is true, because culture is the way men organize themselves and express themselves within that social organization.

Yet a modern Christian and statesman, Senator Mark Hatfield, seems to better tell it like it must be for the Christian in *Conflict and Conscience:*

> The present relationship between the church and pressing social problems here in America disturbs me greatly. For one thing, it tends to keep people whom we might expect to have the highest motivations and the purest concern from becoming actively involved in these problems. The quest for a just social order thus becomes purely secular, and the religious dimension of poverty—the poverty of the human spirit—is neglected while material dimensions of poverty are attacked. The saints of the present are, in the words of Albert Camus, "secular saints."
>
> I tend to disagree with this whole concept of "secular sainthood," for I feel that only the genuinely religious dimension of concern for our fellow-man can overcome the self-interest which characterizes virtually all political activity. But the truth of the matter is that concerned people seem to find little or no support in their churches in the quest they are making for a more just social order. If the church does not want the new order to be purely a secular order—or more important, if the church believes that a secular order . . . ultimately rests on religious and philosophical values—it had better reexamine its relationship to the forces for social justice and betterment in this country and throughout the world.

In other words, the Christian who refuses the conflict risk of involvement with the state is surrendering the goals and destiny of the state to secular forces, by simple default.

If Senator Hatfield's position seems more adequate than that of the isolationist Tertullian, it is also better than that of an acquaintance of mine, who stood at the other end of the spectrum. The man preceded a run for the Senate in his state with a year in very high church office. He wrote a book in which he almost equated service and loyalty to the state with service and loyalty to God. Whereas Tertullian deemed culture and involvement in it as evil, this man seemed to hold that the particular state approaches holiness, and that man is edified by serving it.

Second Timothy 2, again, carries Paul's insight on this count. "A soldier on active service," he told Timothy, "will not let himself be involved in civilian affairs. . . ." That's the way the New English Bible puts verse four. The King James Version of the Bible has it like this: "No man that warreth entangleth himself with the affairs of this life. . . ." To come back to the point of a moment ago, if you are a soldier of the Christ who happens to be working in the affairs of state, then be a soldier of Christ. Don't get tangled in the standards and ideals and practices of that state if it means sacrificing your commitment to Christ.

It's not, as one commentator puts it, that Paul was saying, "Stay aloof." That would contradict what he had said elsewhere. What he was saying was that by duty, the Christian will get involved, but not get entangled to the degree he is ineffectual as a servant of Christ.

Jesus said, in a famous line, "Render therefore unto Caesar the things which are Caesar's; and unto God the things that are God's" (Matthew 22:21 KJV). Assuming, then, that there will be involvement, that the Christian will "render to Caesar," another conflict risk is born: what precisely is it we Christians are to render to Caesar?

For the Christian risking the conflict of getting involved with the state, there are three basic attitudes essential to governing that involvement. Being a disciple—though a poor one—of the art of alliteration, I spell them out like this: The Christian should attempt a prayerful attitude for his state, a praiseful attitude, when it's possible, and a prophetic attitude.

Prayer is the most undersold commodity in the Christian experience. When we come to prayer and government, we think of stage-frightened clergymen reading comma-perfect prayers in great halls occupied by people whose minds are a universe or so away. Or, we think of politicians making a large thing out of public religion, through marketplace prayers, largely for purposes of image.

Okay, there are vast inconsistencies when it comes to prayer and the state.

But what about the responsibility of the Christian to pray for his government? That responsibility carries with it the immense risk of finding out what to pray for. Conflict is born from such.

The Christian finds, often, that there are things he would like changed in government. Prayer being the undersold commodity it is, he sometimes forgets that it may be more powerful than letters to congressmen or even guerilla theater at the White House fence. To paraphrase John Haggai, what would happen if Christians prayed as hard for the Holy Spirit to break into the lives of world leaders as they prayed for the return of the wounded Apollo 13 spacecraft?

Prayer, rising sometimes from that risky conflict, might even be a means of resolving conflict. In Washington, there are prayer groups functioning in the Senate and the House of Representatives. I have seen a liberal Democrat like Iowa's Senator Harold Hughes united in spiritual kinship with a conservative Republican like Senator Strom Thurmond of South Carolina. They've simply found that, while they have their differences on the floor of the Senate, the unity they discover when they turn in prayer to a common Father far transcends those differences.

But not every Christian, of course, is in the Congress. The majority are outside government, which means that <u>that majority, in its risky involvement with the state, must pray for the government</u>.

Nor should that majority assume the people of government don't want it. Indeed, they want it sometimes even when they don't know they do. Our White House prayer group was piddling along with an average attendance of three. We assumed that trying to contact others on the staff would be a waste of time. There were early-morning meetings and all kinds of bureaucratic things, we assumed, to divert them from wanting to pray. But we decided to put out the word there was a prayer-group meeting on Thursdays in the executive dining room of the west wing. Unbelievably, to this then skeptical mind, our attendance swelled to fifteen and twenty through the expedient of a simple memo. It was as if these men, with their sometimes haughty veneer, hungered for communion with God. Maybe I was deluded, but I got to know some of them. And I don't think I was deluded.

If prayer changes things, it can change things in government. And, a prayer of gratitude can be a source of affirmation for those things a government does right.

Despite notions to the contrary, governments get things right on many occasions. That's why the Christian, taking the risks of involvement with his state, must also carry the attitude of praise, or to break out of the alliterative, appreciation.

Plain, open praise, (though not the ultimate kind given to God) can be placed on a nation which rebuilds former enemies to the extent they are its greatest competitors in world trade; to a nation which comes to grips with its previous denial of equal rights for all its people, no matter how agonizing the trip to that point; to a nation that lets itself undergo the free and peaceful revolution of the electorate every four years; to a nation considering 6 percent of its work force too many unemployed.

Those are some of the good things, worthy of praise in American life. But praise can also be a means of helping a nation live up to some of its unfulfilled dreams. The popular notion is that the best way to prod the nation is to adopt the stance of the nagging cynic. Having worked in government, I know how it feels to be told constantly by some that you never can do anything right, and probably never will.

The task of the Christian is to affirm possibility. The Jesus-follower is the one who says, "I know there are giant barriers, and I know that we men are sinful, but through the power of God, one can get the strength to do this thing right." That is holy confidence, and no individual needs it more than governmental types.

Jesus, for example, commanded seventy of His disciples to go out and take the world. Suppose He had said something like this: "You people are such finks that I know all you want out of this is personal reward. The world is too big for you. There's really no way bums like you can do this work. But go out and do it anyway." Look at what Jesus really did. He gathered the messengers, sinners all, but He never stressed that. Rather, He gave them their marching orders, injected them with the confidence-building vision that the message they had was God's, and sent them off. And Luke tells us that they "came back jubilant," announcing that, "In your name, Lord, even the devils submit to us" (Luke 10:17 NEB). The Christian, bearing an affirmative relationship in his risky involvement with his state, can help spur it to a confidence in which it can fulfill its positive goals.

But that means the Christian cannot be a dummy, patting the state on the back for everything it does, and never raising questions. The Christian in such a role simply has no credibility as a Christian. Remember, if you're going to be a soldier of Christ involved in affairs of state, be a soldier of Christ—and that means a Christ-follower taking the prayer-and-praiseful stance must also take the conflict-laden, prophetic attitude with regard to the state.

Simply put: Against the command of Christ, the Christian should measure the ethics and morality by which his state behaves, and when it strays, the Christian must call it to that higher standard.

When the church has abdicated this prophetic role with regard to its governing power, it has always lost its witness. The church in the medieval period, for example, saw the state largely as an extension of itself, when in reality, the church deteriorated to merely an extension of the state. Kings became chief bishops on the strength of their political offices. The church became corrupt; religion was a form of pledging allegiance to the state. What resulted was a "dark age."

In Nazi Germany, the state church became a mime of the Nazi state. And the underground, confessing church, in which Bonhoeffer and his friends ministered, sprang up to keep alive the witness of Christ.

In Western society—particularly the United States—it is

critical that the church (which is the Christian who is the church in the world) blend the prophetic attitude with those of prayer and praise, because, in America at least, there is the tendency to assume that this is a nation raised up by God Himself. And from that premise it is easy to assume, therefore, that whatever the state does is right. Senator Hatfield, in *Conflict and Conscience,* recalls for us de Tocqueville's idea:

> It must never be forgotten that religion gave birth to Anglo-American society. In the United States, religion is therefore mingled with all the habits of the nation and all the feelings of patriotism, whence it derives a peculiar force.

Wrong or right, nations of the world often think we Americans think of ourselves as having sprung full-grown from the head of a god. And that's a major reason Christians can't keep their mouths shut when it comes to matters of state. What's at stake is our credibility as witnesses of Christ! If the Third World, for example, has the idea that we Christians think we have a monopoly on God's wisdom and spirit, what kind of witness are we projecting through national policy, in our collective acts as American people? You and I know that our leaders seldom if ever hack out policy before an altar, and those people to whom we want to aim our witness (as we aim it at ourselves) know it too. But they don't know that we know it. We are sinful, as are all other nations. *But what they think we think we are,* and what Christians in the prophetic role know us to be in actuality are two different things. It would be lovely to write off the rest of the world, some think. Their feeling is that America has done enough for everybody, and we can just, in a well-known metaphor, let the world twist slowly in the wind. But no responsible Christian can take such an attitude, mainly because of the devastating consequences on the attempt to share the gospel.

The prophetic role, with all its risk of conflict, has a domestic as well as an international slant. There is too often, on the part of the people who manage to get themselves in charge, the tendency to conclude that if America's foundations are basically religious, and they are the leaders of this religious-based nation, they therefore have the right to use whatever means available to keep power. Perhaps Watergate was the monstrous child of this notion, which has been around long enough to set up housekeeping with the American political system. The Christian, in his prophetic stance, must challenge this idea, reminding leaders that they, too, are sinners before God, and stand in need of redemption as much as anybody else.

The Christian risking the conflict of the prophetic role must never employ the same tactics of violence and abuse some secular critics use. During one of the bloodiest episodes in the tearing saga of Northern Ireland, I attended a conference on Christian morality, in London. Europeans were there from all over. But the fellow who latched heaviest on my conscience was a Belfast accountant I'll call Kevin O'Leary. We were staying in a ruddy, old lodge at Windsor Great Park. It was summer, and the royal family was in residence at Windsor. One evening after a conference session, Kevin and I went walking beneath the twisted, ancient oaks. I was talking, and in his wry, Irish humor, Kevin was whispering, "Be quiet, or you'll wake the queen."

I had been drawn to Kevin because, earlier in the day, conversation had drifted, in the conference, to Northern

Ireland's travail. One continental European had pulled himself up to full snobbery, and chastened the behavior of the "Christians" in Northern Ireland. All the colors of the spectrum exploded on Kevin's face as he struggled not to let his mouth explode in rebuttal. At last he was in charge. Calmly, he looked at Monsieur Pious, and said, "But those are not the real Christians." No, they're not, I thought. It is not for the Christian to sling fire bombs and gut buildings and practice butchery to get across his prophetic point!

Colin Morris, a British clergyman with much frustrating and agonizing service in Africa, might not agree, in part anyway. In his book *Unyoung, Uncolored, Unpoor,* he says:

> Yes, I believe a Christian is justified in using violence to win freedom in Rhodesia. . . . I believe freedom fighters are justified in using any methods short of sadistic cruelty for its own sake to overthrow the Salisbury regime.

But why draw the line at "sadistic cruelty for its own sake"? If one secular behavior pattern is to be adopted, why not throw off all the restrictions? If the Christian perspective is to be scrapped in part, why not scrap it altogether? Morris, a critic of American involvement in Vietnam (about which he may have been right; that is not the point) seems to be ensnared in contradiction. If the Christian perspective can be scrapped in Rhodesia, why can't the South Vietnamese, with American assistance, scrap it to fend off the North Vietnamese? Morris's dilemma is typical of what happens when the Christian tries to adapt to the world's methodologies.

That is part of the risk of conflict: the Christian is called to put everything on methods and strategies the world smirks at and labels as ineffective and inane. But the point is, in his conflict, be it with others, his culture in general, or his government, the Christian comes at it from the Christ perspective, so much so that even those in the secular world who momentarily consider themselves his allies, may wind up thinking the Christian is out of it!

To be a follower of Jesus, then, is to risk being caught up in all kinds of conflict. This being the case, why is it that Jesus and the Bible writers made such a big thing of peace? In Romans 5, for example, Paul is emphatic that, since we have been reconciled to God through Christ, we have peace with God.

But Jesus gives the clue to the unraveling of the paradox between peace and conflict when He says that He gives peace, but "not as the world giveth . . ." (John 14:27 KJV). The world looks at peace as the absence of conflict. Jesus' kind of peace comes in the midst of conflict. It is the peace of personal security, the assurance that even in the bonfire, there is a cool, protective breeze. The Christ-follower knows that his soul is clenched tightly in the strong hand of Jesus. He knows that "neither death, nor life, nor angels, nor principalities, nor powers, nor things present, nor things to come, Nor height, nor depth, nor any other creature, shall be able to separate us from the love of God, which is in Christ Jesus our Lord" (Romans 8:38,39 KJV).

Thus the peace of God is an intimate thing—something of the soul, in which the disciple is in the protective (and liberating) custody of his Master. The deeper he plunges into a relationship with Christ, the more intense grows the conflict, and the more sweeping the peaceful knowledge that despite all the blood, sweat, and tears, nothing can disrupt the chain of love, tied to his buffeted spirit, and anchored in the heart of God!

7

THE RISK OF GOING ALL THE WAY

Being a good American who believes that mustard and catsup outrank protoplasm as the stuff of life, I am expert in the various ways of ordering a hot dog. My favorite contralto is a wispy lady in a snack shop on Third Avenue in Birmingham who, on taking an order for a hot dog, cries, "Load one!" I am, therefore, almost sickened when some persnickety soul enters the sandwich establishment and asks the lady to hold the mustard, or the onions, or the kraut. It is a crime, a denial of the whole; for the hot dog "all the way" is a wondrous unity, and to deprive it of any of its parts is to shatter the symmetry.

Surprisingly, there are those who like their salvation like their hot dogs: in fractions. It is as if one could go to God and say, "Lord, give me your salvation, but hold the crucifixion." For such folk, redemption is a flexible ware, coming in the deluxe and regular versions. And they wonder why on earth anyone would ever want the brand with the inconvenience of crucifixion when they can get the deluxe style, and avoid the cross!

But salvation does not come in bits and pieces. It comes "all the way," as a whole, and to be a disciple of Christ means to be, as Paul said it, "crucified with him" (Romans

6:6 KJV). In fact, in this chapter, we won't be talking about crucifixion as some chancy risk, but as inevitability. The risks we shall discuss are those which cling to crucifixion like parasite fishes to a shark.

John Cheever's novel *Bullet Park* is the description of life in an affluent, outwardly placid suburb. The people belong to the church much as they do the country club. But the religion of Bullet Park cannot tolerate the slightest hint of crucifixion. Cheever gives us an inside look at one of his noncrucified churchgoers during a morning worship service:

> His sense of the church calendar was much more closely associated with the weather than with the revelations and strictures in the Holy Gospel. St. Paul meant blizzards. St. Matthias meant a thaw. For the marriage at Cana and the cleansing of the leper the oil furnace would still be running although the vents in the stained-glass windows were sometimes open to the raw spring air. . . . Jesus departs from the coasts of Tyre and Sidon as the skiing ends. For the crucifixion a bobsled stands stranded in a flowerbed, its painter coiled among the early violets. The trout streams open for the resurrection.

It sounds sacrilegious. But the characteristic of the uncrucified quasi Christianity is that the cross is not permitted to loom with its demands and pain, even in the midst of a church service—and that is sacrilege.

What are the elements of the uncrucified, Bullet Park religion? Certainly a major bolt in this flimsy structure is that of convenience. Uncrucified, Bullet Park faith is terribly convenient. We are a culture of "convenience" stores,

"convenience" appliances, instant breakfasts, and pack-
aged love, and we have grown to expect convenient and
easy redemption. Within this expectation, a religion has
been concocted that is capable of having its dogma bent
and stretched to fit whatever demands easy faith makes. In
the process we have succeeded in running off from our
churches many of those who believe that real religion carries with it the pain of a cross.

Conservatives, with their exuberance to bend the practice of faith with surrounding culture, have helped to
shape Bullet Park religion. But the liberals, wanting to
charge out the gate and into battle just about the time
secular tribes have littered the battlefields with bodies and
pitched their rest tents, have made a major contribution to
building the uncrucified religion of fashion, if not convenience.

Bishop John A.T. Robinson, known as the bishop of
Woolwich (in England), and famous for, among other things,
his *Honest to God,* perhaps unwittingly is an example. "If
the church is to travel sufficiently light," he has said in Joe
David Brown's *Can Christianity Survive?* "and to be flexible for a mobile society organized on functional lines, then
it must be free to deploy most of its manpower not for
servicing units of the ecclesiastical plant but for serving
. . . the world."

I couldn't agree more that the church should shift its focus
from greasing the wheels of its own structure simply for the
sake of greasing the wheels. I am an avid supporter of the
idea held by Bishop Robinson (who, incidentally, is echoing
what scores of evangelicals are saying, from Findley Edge to
Carl F.H. Henry and Sherwood Wirt), that the thrust of our
servanthood should be toward the world. But much of the

problem of the modern church is that it is already "too light." It is simply bending itself out of shape sometimes because it is so "flexible."

A "functional society" is one organized on lines of pragmatism and practicality. Contrary to what the bishop says, the last thing in the world (and for the world's sake) the church needs to do is parody its society and twist itself into a holy pretzel someone will label as "functional." To be "functional" in this sense would imply acquiescence to that centrality around which secular culture functions. That would amount to secular syncretism. A church which asks its people to believe nothing absolute, to commit to nothing absolute, to be guided by nothing absolute, is indeed "light" and mobile. But it also happens to be stagnant and incapable of a unique and refreshing ministry to the world. If one can have the convenience of melting dogma and strictures of faith and pouring the molten stuff into a man-made mold, why should he surrender to the inconvenience of serving the world? Bishop Robinson has it backwards: Before we Christians can lay it all on the line in the world, we've got to lay on the cross all our petty penchants to sculpt a religion of convenience!

Even at that, I think Bishop Robinson misunderstands the organization of society. It is not necessarily organized around function. To have a function hints at the existence of ends and goals, something the function is designed to achieve. In fact, function is defined in terms of its aims. But secular culture seems to be caught up in the chaos noted wryly by Einstein when he said that we seem to have all sorts of means for getting places, we just don't know where we're going. Rather than being a "functional society," we are a "utilitarian society." The temptation hurled at the

Christian in such a culture is for him to adapt to the utilitarian mode.

Basically, says Webster, utilitarianism is the doctrine "that the aim of action is the largest possible balance of pleasure over pain." This is precisely what the crucifixionless religion of Bullet Park is all about. It is a utilitarian faith that will meld with our pleasurable but strangely unhappy society. The church of Bullet Park may as well change its sign to read FIRST UTILITARIAN CHURCH. The preference of this religion without crucifixion is for the sideshow, the doings of magic. It rallies at its Lourdes, but skirts Golgotha; it plants and gilds tabernacles in Utopia, but gets the AAA to map it around Samaria.

This was what all the fuss about "relative ethics" was all about. It turned out that it wasn't a relative ethic being brewed in the semantic pot as much as it was a utilitarian ethic. Midst pompous pronouncements about the need for a "new morality" was the same old sordid truth—that we want resurrection without crucifixion, the game without the blame. The Brahmins of the new morality never caught the point that a utilitarian ethic is as wrong when it stretches to suit total permissiveness in sexual mores as it was when it was adapted to a morality permitting slavery. After all, the preachers who pounded their pulpits in defense of slavery during the Civil War and before were no different, in this respect at least, than today's ethical utilitarians who sermonize us suavely ad infinitum and nauseum from slick magazine pages like Hugh Hefner's *Playboy,* and from movies like Bertolucci's *Last Tango.*

"Hold the crucifixion"-type religion is not only convenient; it is also fashionable. Religion is "in" at the moment. It's the thing with everybody from the Process church folk

I saw on Bourbon Street a while back, to the Hare Krishna people whom I watched clang their ringlets in front of the White House. Even the Bullet Park folk are finding church-going as fashionable as it has ever been. Theodore Roszak, the Melanchthon of the counterculture, spends 465 pages in *Where the Wasteland Ends* telling us religion is likely to strike next in politics. *Jesus Christ Superstar* is a brilliant theater marquee (the Lord's name is at last up in lights); Paul McCartney joins with Simon and Garfunkel and Judy Collins in a rock choir of sorts, spinning out tunes with definite mystical overtones. "Amazing Grace" has hit the charts and gone off the scale.

And the cross—its popularity is right up there with bell-bottoms and Levis. There seems something askew with this turning of the cross into an art object. Yet there it is, dangling in the cleavage of an X-rated starlet as she earns her bread. We even co-opt the cross to symbolize our secular brain-children, to represent our movements and causes. It isn't the first time, of course; Hitler merely bent it a bit. And Herbert Gilmore recalls, in *When Love Prevails,* what a man told him once: "The trouble with you Christians is that you wear the cross, but you don't get on it."

What's ironic is that the practitioners of uncrucified religion consider themselves mortal enemies, squatting on opposite ends of the pole. But really they are soul brothers (in a spiritual sense, of course). For example, the Bullet Park types commit adultery, like Mrs. Robinson, in their hidden boudoirs or closets. The uncrucified, but fashionably "into religion" folk of the counterculture commit their adultery in communes and at Woodstock and Watkins Glen (claiming some special dispensation because they do it "honestly," which means in the open). But both would feel equally put out if someone suggested that real religion means you put the flesh to death on a cross so that the spirit might have vitality. But the uncrucified followers of camp religion have many ancestors. One of them, an English nobleman of a century or so ago, told it like it is for them all. "Things have come to a pretty pass," he said, "when religion is allowed to interfere with a man's private life." Fashionable, un-crucified religion, of course, interferes with neither the pri-vate nor the public life of its disciple. It doesn't want for takers.

What will happen when the cycle of fashion spins around again, as it probably will, and religion is no longer the sport-ing thing? The historical record is downright depressing. In the eighteenth century, for example, England experienced one of those fiery, authentic revivals, under men like the Wesleys. In the twentieth century, Britain is a spiritual bed case, with many churches deserted, the country waffling along from one moral impasse to another. And despite the fashionableness of cultural religion in America, political dis-ease festers.

What really happens is this: Real revival brings real reli-gion and real religion demands crucifixion and crucifixion weeds the harvest. The first to go are those for whom faith has been a fashionable ploy. One doesn't climb the cross for the sake of appearances! So it may be that the criteria of real revival should not be in mass statistics, but in the founding of some small cells of people who are committed to a thoroughly unfashionable brand of faith "all the way." "The gospel," says Elton Trueblood, "conquers the world by the establishment of small strong points."

Those looking for the deluxe, crucifixionless brand of salvation are more in search of salve than salvation. They want the religion of Huxley's *Brave New World*—"Christianity without tears." There is a balance between suffering and salving in the Christian faith. But for the follower of Bullet Park religion, God is more grandfather than father. He chuckles over the clever deviousness of His people. The message in Hebrews—that God sometimes chastens His real sons and daughters—is sliced from the Scripture.

To the Bullet Park religious types who have a hard time identifying with a grandfather image, God is the divine nanny. He is paid to bear the responsibility of keeping the charge twittering with glee. The divine nanny showers His little person with goodies, and when rain threatens, always sees to it that the little one is sheltered safely.

If neither grandfather nor divine nanny will do to suggest the god of uncrucified religion, try Santa Claus, or the fairy godmother, or the good witch of the west, or any other symbol of a doting do-gooder whose only interest is in working magic, even if genuine love calls for something else. For what this god of the uncrucified religion really is, is a divine rationalizer. That's why his religion is so soothing: it is an easy instrument for providing justification for anything a person wants to do. It is also why it knows nothing of crucifixion.

Thus, you can have religion without crucifixion—but you can't have life. It may seem odd, but life in Christ begins at the place of death. ". . . he that loseth his life for my sake shall find it," said Jesus (Matthew 10:39 KJV). Paul echoes, "I am crucified with Christ: nevertheless I live . . ." (Galatians 2:20 KJV). And I love Carlyle Marney's definition of death in *Faith in Conflict:* becoming.

Crucifixion is the prerequisite for life for the simple reason that what passes for life in the precrucified person is counterfeit. More than that, precrucifixion existence is a distortion, a caricature of what life can become in Christ. Whatever else Adam's sin in Eden meant, it provided the opportunity for Satan to substitute genuine life with artificiality. Existence without Christ is a plastic flower. It glimmers and smiles on the outside, but it is a facade. This counterfeit existence has to be put to death if genuine life is to come.

A few years ago, Miss America came to town. I was committing that ultimate stupidity in a newspaper city room, sitting at my desk doing nothing. The city editor noted I was idle, and decided I would cover the arrival of the lady. I went to the airport and found the room scheduled for the press conference. In a sweep of taut, puffy hair and luscious perfume, Miss America came on stage. The lady announced she had come to town to address a youth conference, to give the kids some tips on how to live. I thought it a good idea to ask her views on the subject. "What do you believe to be the purpose of life?" I asked. "Why, why . . . to be happy," said she, midst wilting hair spray. "But to what end?" I queried, my reportorial blood beginning to pump with a little more zest. "Just to be happy," said the nation's loveliest.

To give the girl due credit, I concluded that what she was talking about was self-fulfillment. Indeed, this seems to be the *raison d'être* for the bulk of humanity who are free enough from the labors of survival to contemplate the meaning of selfhood.

Jose Ortega Y Gasset, the Spanish philosopher, is quoted in *Man and People* as having said, "Life is a permanent crossroads, a constant perplexity," because man is the only creature who must choose his own being. But in the uncrucified state, man's search for himself is the attempt to penetrate a primeval jungle in which paths have not yet been hacked out. And, in the uncrucified being, it is to enter this jungle without the one Guide who knows the way to the explorer's destination.

For example, in his quest for self-realization, man probes about for something called "humanity." "To be more human" is the way he states his goal. But there are too many characteristics claiming to be the definers of real humanity. For one person, genuine humanity lies in the acquisition of power, or the ability to dominate others. Yet for others, to be fully human might mean to resist that power, to be a revolutionary, or at least a rebel. Which, then, is the real humanity toward which all men should move? Sammy Davis used to croon, "I Gotta Be Me." But in the uncrucified man, that is the problem: What is me?

Malachi Martin, in his book *The Encounter,* tries to point up the ways he feels the major religions have failed mankind. Sometimes he uses a fictionalized form to make his point. In one chapter, the world is at the abyss of nuclear holocaust. As a last-ditch effort, leaders of the world's faiths gather at a religious summit to try to plot a map to peace. What they wind up with is a declaration of sorts, which starts like this: "The purpose of our common action is to act as men, with men, for men's sake, and according to the destiny of men." It is well that Martin's example is fiction. For—and the question harks back to the Psalmist and before —what is man? And, more importantly—what does man *mean?*

The only way to get at the answer is to begin putting things to death. Elements of life which deprive man of his full potential must be hung on a cross. But our daily experience in the Naked City shows us that for all our effort, we are still far more skilled in finding ways to dehumanize than in discovering what real humanity is. We have become as skilled at making masks as those characters on "Mission Impossible." The rubbery substance of the masks moves and creases. They can smile and weep, and after a while we forget which are masks and which is really us. Yet the only way we can realize self genuinely is to put the sham to death.

Findley Edge, author of *The Greening of the Church,* catches the dilemma of self-realization through "becoming more fully human." The Bible, he reminds us, talks, not of being "more human," but of a "new humanity." In its uncrucified state, humanity is in disorder, and, says Edge, from that perspective to "become more fully human" is to simply amplify disorder. Thus, in the absence of the crucifixion which kills the elements blocking man from becoming the "new being," the quest to "become more fully human" is a deceitful, futile exercise.

Considered apart from Christ, this is a pretty bleak conclusion. One would be tempted to join Camus and Sartre in their depressing hopelessness. But the good news is that it is possible for man to achieve "self-realization," "identity," and "humanity" in the sense they were designed by his Creator! And the way to come alive is through death.

Few struggling, up-against-the-wall people have grasped this fact more thoroughly than Saul of Tarsus, the fellow we know as the Apostle Paul. He lays it all out in Philippians 3:4-11:

> If anyone thinks to base his claims on externals, I could make a stronger case for myself: circumcised on my eighth day, Israelite by race, of the tribe of Benjamin, a Hebrew

born and bred; in my attitude to the law, a Pharisee; in
pious zeal, a persecutor of the church; in legal rectitude,
faultless. But all such assets I have written off because of
Christ. I would say more: I count everything sheer loss,
because all is far outweighed by the gain of knowing Christ
Jesus my Lord, for whose sake I did in fact lose everything.
I count it so much garbage, for the sake of gaining Christ
and finding myself incorporate in him, with no righteousness of my own, no legal rectitude, but the righteousness
which comes from faith in Christ, given by God in response
to faith. All I care for is to know Christ, to experience the
power of his resurrection, and to share his sufferings, in
growing conformity with his death, if only I may finally
arrive at the resurrection from the dead.

NEB

If pedigree is self-realization, Saul had it! Prior to his
encounter with Christ, he had certainly found something he
concluded was "himself." In the passage just quoted, Paul
goes to some lengths to make clear he thought he had
selfhood tied up in a neat box. He was a true Israelite, not
a proselyte. No, sir, Saul was the real McCoy, belonging to
the stock of Jacob. What's more, Saul had been "of the tribe
of Benjamin," that fierce little band that gave Israel its first
king (also a man named Saul), and which always had the
place of honor in war. Saul considered himself a model, a
"Hebrew of the Hebrews." Using a word his people hung
on themselves when in slavery and exile, he showed his
identity was total. Saul was the son of a Pharisee, but he had
also made a conscious choice to be a Pharisee. It was no
ho-hum thing with him. He studied Pharisaism doggedly, at
the school of Hillel, at the feet of Gamaliel, who was to

Pharisaism what Newton was to physics. He followed the law to the tiniest jot, and was so zealous he went hounding after the church like a rabid wolf. This guy was playing for keeps, and if anyone had stopped young Saul of Tarsus on the street and asked him if he had an identity problem, he would have broken up at the absurdity of the question.

But abruptly all this was as meaningless to Paul as if Saul had been some cartoon character drawn and then erased by the artist. Suddenly he blurted, So what! "But all such assets I have written off because of Christ." There is the smell of death here. Something has been hung on a cross, and it appears to be what once passed for Paul's selfhood. "This is no momentary impulse, no spasmodic rhapsody on Paul's part," said A.T. Robertson in *Paul's Joy in Christ*. "Here he takes his stand. This is his choice in life." So Paul says that his counterfeit selfhood was the vilest garbage imaginable. It was as repugnant to him as that World War II nerve gas that had to be disposed of several years ago. The stuff was so horrid that the states through which it would pass to its ocean dumping ground went ape in protest. Paul says his old selfhood, once a treasury of personal assets, is now *skubala*, dung, vile, abhorrent, worthless.

So Paul has come to the mouth of *gehenna*, the garbage dump, stripped off what he once thought to be his identity, and hurled it in. He has hitched a rope to Saul of Tarsus and dragged him up Golgotha, the place of the skull, and put him to death on a cross. There is no more Saul of Tarsus. Even the name is lost. Paul has passed the Failsafe point; he is committed to whatever lies ahead. There can be no turning back. Where does he go now for his identity, his self-realization? He tells us, "All I care for is to know Christ, to experience the power of his resurrection, and to share his sufferings, in growing conformity with his death, if only I may finally arrive at the resurrection from the dead."

Thus Paul was at the heart of a concept uniquely his own: he was "in Christ," and in that state Paul had his own self-potential affirmed. Paul, having put Saul to death, and now being in Christ, was free at last to become what Paul could. He was a slave, but marvelously free—free to *become*. "I am crucified with Christ: nevertheless I live; yet not I, but Christ liveth in me. . . ." Paul says in Galatians 2:20 (KJV). "The life principle which was Paul is dead; and Christ has become the life principle in him," writes William Barclay in *The Mind of St. Paul.*

It makes sense. If, as stated already in another chapter, Jesus is the *Logos,* the Power behind creation, then it is clear He is the Power behind life. If He *made* man, then He is capable of *enabling* man to realize his full potential as a self. Stanley Kubrick's *2001: A Space Odyssey* illustrates the point. The dream of man since Eden has been to unravel the secrets of the universe. It is achieved in *2001* (and thereby we know it is fiction). An astronaut, lost in space, undergoes some weird metamorphosis and becomes a fetus, carried in the womb of the cosmos. He is the child of the universe, and because he is *in* creation as if merged into it, he comprehends it. So to be *in* Christ is to be merged with the very principle of our being. Tillich's description of God as the "Ground of all being" may not go far enough. Yet God is the ground, or foundation of our selfhood, and to be in Christ is to be immersed in what we are to become. Even in *2001,* the astronaut has to disappear so that the fetus may appear. To be in Christ, and hence in the very womb of life's ultimate essence, the partial, incomplete, artificial self has to die.

Unamuno, the Spanish Christian, got the point. A sculptor had been molding a statue of the philosopher. One morning the artist came back to his unfinished work, took the damp cloths from the clay, and found that Unamuno had slipped into the studio during the night and done his own sculpting. Over the heart of the statue, Unamuno, with his finger as a chisel, had dug out a cross. One of the most dramatic and promising messages of the Good News is that the ugly cross has been transformed into the symbol of life. The sign which once spooked men into scampering away is now the welcome mat—but a welcome mat with not-so-fine print, reading: WELCOME TO REAL LIFE—but enter at your own risk.

Anybody who gets mixed up with a cross risks being considered a colossal failure. There is even evidence that Jesus' disciples, before his Resurrection, concluded that the Lord had blown it. Between Friday and Sunday of that horrid weekend, they were as scarce as gangsters at a policemen's ball. We know that John was off caring for Jesus' mother. But where was that loudmouth, Simon Peter? What about the egotistical social climbers, James and John? Had anyone seen Matthew, the tax collector, or Thomas, or Andrew, or any of the rest of Jesus' crew? We can only conclude that they were off somewhere sweating it out, wondering where to go from here. Those who were around were the women, but they had only come to care for a dead body. It seems no one was expecting Resurrection. They must have concluded that Jesus was no more than a bungler.

It is so now as well. Anyone who lets himself be crucified with Christ is going to get stuck with a failure sign around his neck as glaring as the Ancient Mariner's albatross. But did you ever see a "failure" smile? Behind the tears of the

Crucifixion was the glimmering smile of Resurrection. Besides, I have an uncle who proves that a crucified "failure" has a much greater edge on meaning and joy than an uncrucified "success." Uncle Redus Vasser, by the standards of "making it," has not. He's been in a state called retirement longer than I can remember. But it's only semantical retirement. Halfway through his life, he heard the voice of God tumbling through his being, calling him to the ministry, professionally. Few men climb on the cross Uncle Redus mounted. He nailed and killed his seniority and pulled the slats from under his growing government pension. Now he lives in a little house in Pensacola, and he sits on the same furniture he sat on thirty years ago and has turnip greens for lunch. But if he's a failure, he doesn't know it. In fact, he considers himself quite the opposite. A while back, he wrote me a letter: " . . . when we find ourselves so committed to the way of life that we lose all expectations of self-gratitude, we gain life. The rhythm of our life moves in step with the Divine beat." Men have killed themselves because they didn't have the self-fulfillment Uncle Redus has!

Nevertheless, the world wastes no time in hanging out the wreaths for the crucified. To be crucified with Christ means that one is going to risk looking like he's finished, *kaput*. To come back to the point of a moment ago, the women at Jesus' tomb were there with ointment for a *dead* body. Despite Lazarus and all those others who were dead but who were now alive, the conclusion was that Jesus had had it. Nowadays when you get crucified with Christ, you're going to risk having your name stricken off the lists at your former hangouts. Old acquaintances may treat you as if you are a walking zombie.

It happened to Mr. Magic. He was the best and maybe

only hillbilly magician in existence. He would sally up to his magician's table with all the mystery of an oriental fakir, his head twined in a turban, but immediately would dash it all when he opened his mouth and out tumbled south Alabama. Mr. Magic did a television show, and the kids loved him. But after a while, Mr. Magic faded, and I was wondering what ever happened to him. One day at the television studio where I occasionally worked, I heard an engineer ask another what had happened to Mr. Magic. "Oh, he got religion," the fellow replied, with all the morbidity of a man who had just seen a hearse. As far as they were concerned, Mr. Magic was finished as a magician, and as a human being as well.

But crucifixion is not a conclusion. It is denouement, that ultimate point to which people must move if they're to have life. Christianity is that paradoxical and wonderful faith that makes synonymous beginnings and endings. The prime Christian word for end is *eschaton*. But *eschaton* is not the final slam of the vault, nor the sealing of the tomb. *Eschaton* means goal, purpose, a destination. It is wrapped up with resurrection.

In the Philippians passage quoted earlier, Paul lets us know he hasn't reached the fullness of that selfhood that comes with crucifixion and resurrection. "But," he says, "I press on, hoping to take hold of that for which Christ once took hold of me . . . forgetting what is behind me, and reaching out for that which lies ahead, I press towards the goal to win the prize which is God's call to the life above, in Christ Jesus" (verses 12–14 NEB).

No man reaches out "for that which lies ahead" unless he is a fool or has confidence that something good is out there. No, the crucified Christ-disciple shouldn't be written

off as finished; he is a person moving toward the realization
of what his life is all about, and he got started on the trip
using a cross as a launching pad!

I wish others could see this!

Maybe in the childlike simplicity of a story like *Snow White and the Seven Dwarfs* lies a hint of the mysterious working of God in merging our beginnings and ends. Everyone knows the story: the lovely girl comes to live in the forest with the overworked elves; the wicked witch gets upset because her mirror has an embarrassing attachment to the child, and so the old woman decides to kill her with a poisoned apple. The apple is pawned off on Snow White; she eats it and dies. The dwarfs come home and weep while the kids in the theater sniffle. But Hallelujah! Comes Prince Charming, plants a kiss on the ivory cheek of Snow White, and life is restored.

That is precisely what it is to be a Christian: it is to risk an encounter with the witch, to eat the poisoned apple by climbing a cross. But it is to soar through life with the grand assurance that no matter how bloody the crucifixion, no matter how bleak the outlook of appearances, no matter how stark the risks, always, the Prince will come!